Rob Renfroe

A Way Through the
WILDERNESS

Growing in Faith When Life Is Hard

Nashville
Abingdon Press

A Way Through the Wilderness:
Growing in Faith When Life Is Hard

Copyright © 2015 by Abingdon Press
All rights reserved.

This book is printed on elemental chlorine-free paper.
ISBN 978-1-5018-0095-5

15 16 17 18 19 20 21 22 23 24 — 10 9 8 7 6 5 4 3 2 1
MANUFACTURED IN THE UNITED STATES OF AMERICA

Contents

Introduction 5

1. No Way Around the Wilderness 9

2. Entering the Wilderness 29

3. Walking with Others in the Wilderness 51

4. Walking with God in the Wilderness 75

5. Avoiding Wrong Turns in the Wilderness 99

6. Coming Out of the Wilderness 123

Notes 142

Introduction

My friend asked me how I was doing. "Not that great," I said. He and I had become close friends a few years earlier when God used each of us in the other's life—me to bring him into a relationship with Christ and him to be an encourager in my life. Over time we became as close as brothers.

I had moved to a new community and was serving a church there. I loved the people, but I was frustrated that we weren't growing or moving forward as quickly as I had hoped we would. Looking back on that time in my life, I realize now that my biggest struggle wasn't with the church but with myself—my expectations, self-worth, insecurity, and tendency to equate numerical success with God's blessing.

My friend had called to see how he could pray for me. Because I trusted him and knew that he loved me, I was honest when he asked how life was going. I told him, "I'm frustrated, discontent, discouraged. My energy level is down. People have failed me. My problems seem bigger than I am. And nothing I do seems to make any difference. Other than that, life is great."

"You're going through a wilderness," he responded.

"Of course I'm going through a wilderness," I said. "That's what I just told you. Life is crummy right now."

What he said next sent me on a journey that changed and deepened how I understand what it means to walk with God.

"No, not wilderness as in 'life is crummy right now' but wilderness as in the Bible," he replied. "A spiritual wilderness. You're the preacher, dude. Figure it out."

I took my friend's challenge as a word from the Lord and decided to study the Bible to learn what it means to be in a wilderness. As I did, I asked God these questions:

> What is a wilderness?
> Why do people end up there?
> What are we supposed to learn when we're there?
> How can we learn those lessons quickly so we can get out of the wilderness as soon as possible?

What God taught me through my study not only changed how I see the spiritual life and what it means to walk in faith; it changed me.

My first discovery was that the term *wilderness* is used nearly three hundred times in the Scriptures. We find it in some of the Bible's most critical moments. Abraham decides to follow God's calling upon his life, and he is led into the wilderness. Moses encounters God and receives his calling to deliver the Israelites from bondage in the wilderness. When the Israelites leave Egypt and head to the Promised Land, first they must pass through the wilderness. David learns to trust God in the wilderness, and there he is prepared to fight Goliath and lead Israel. Immediately after Jesus is baptized in the Jordan River, the Spirit drives him into the wilderness for forty days to be tested and tempted by the evil one. Only after this wilderness experience is Jesus ready to begin his ministry and change the world.

Not only was I amazed to learn how often God's people went through a wilderness experience; I began to see that these experiences were important, even necessary, for these people to be prepared to do God's will and fulfill his plan for their lives. I discovered that the wilderness is a training ground God uses to deepen our trust in him and remake our character into the image of his Son. Some lessons about who God is and how we are to walk with him can be learned only when life is difficult and dry—when depending on

God is the only way we will make it. Some truths we know in our heads can become real in our hearts only when we spend time in the wilderness.

As I continued my study, I began to wonder if what I was going through was more than a time of frustration and depression. Perhaps God was at work in my life, making me more like Jesus and teaching me how to walk in faith and minister grace and truth the way that he did. Maybe instead of looking at everything I thought was going wrong around me, I needed to look for what God wanted to do within me. Thinking about my wilderness in this new way did not make it go away. It didn't instantly lift my spirits or change my situation. But it did give me hope. And it did something else just as important: it took my focus off of myself and put it on God. I came to see that God isn't so much a "problem-fixer" as he is a "life-changer." Rather than swooping in to take our problems away, more often he works to change who we are through the problems and the pain of our lives.

All of us go through difficult times. Perhaps you're in a wilderness right now. If so, my heart goes out to you. Some mild wilderness experiences are simply unpleasant. But most feel unbearable. They involve immense suffering and deep sorrow. Often they bring us to the breaking point, if not physically then emotionally and spiritually. Whether it's the loss of a loved one, a financial or health crisis, divorce, or some other painful experience, we see no end in sight and wonder how we can make it through another day. I've had that kind of wilderness experience too. I know what it's like for the night to be dark and the road to be long, when all you have to hold on to are questions without answers. I know what it's like to feel that it's not worth going on—to think my life will never get better and the pain will never end. I know what it's like to question all you believe. I've been there. I understand.

This is my plea: *Don't waste your wilderness*. Don't go through such pain only to gain nothing from it. You will come through your wilderness. The question is, *Who will you be when this difficult time is over?* This is important: it's impossible to go through the wilderness without being changed. How you handle the most difficult times of your life will make you a different person. Make the wrong choices and you may step out of the wilderness broken and bitter and far away from God. But there's a way through the wilderness that will make you stronger, leave you with a deeper faith, and draw you closer to God than you ever imagined.

That is the focus of this book—finding a way through the wilderness so that when you come out, you are more like Jesus than when you went in. It won't be easy. The way of real transformation never is. But I can promise you that it will be worth it. In the light of eternity, we will agree with what the Apostle Paul told the Romans: "I consider that our present sufferings are not worth comparing with the glory that will be revealed in us" (Romans 8:18).

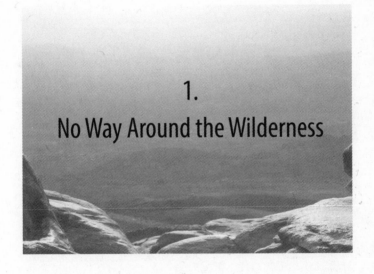

1.
No Way Around the Wilderness

1.

No Way Around the Wilderness

If the wilderness is to have any benefit in our lives, we need to understand what it is, who ends up there, and why God allows us to go through such difficult experiences. The answers to these questions may change not only your understanding of the wilderness but also how you see God.

What Is the Wilderness?

What images come to mind when you think of a wilderness? I'm a Texan, so I think of the heavily forested area in the southeast part of the state known as "The Big Thicket." (It's Texas, so naturally it has to be big, right?) Perhaps the term *wilderness* causes you to think of the magnificent beauty of the great northwest or the towering majesty of the Rocky Mountains, which my wife and I have enjoyed hiking for many years.

Time in the wilderness for most of us means looking for a pair of boots that have been waiting for us in the back of a closet or perhaps making a quick trip to an outdoor specialty store to purchase hiker-chic apparel that makes us look the part. We put some granola bars in a backpack, fill up a water bottle, jump into our vehicle, and head out to enjoy a relaxing day renewed by cool air, the sound of running streams, and the wonders of nature.

Nothing could be further from what the Bible has in mind when it talks about the wilderness. Many Hebrew words are used to describe the various wilderness references we find in the Bible. Common root meanings are *deserted, dry, barren, desolate. Yeshimon* or *Jeshimon* is the name commonly given to the Judean wilderness, which can be translated as "the horror" or "the devastation."[1] If you have been to the Holy Land and have seen the wilderness there, you know how fitting those names are. The ground is hard and dry, consisting of baked sand and limestone. Rainfall is negligible. Water is almost nonexistent. Vegetation is sparse. As far as you can see, the only movement you can detect is the heat shimmering off the desert floor. The air is so hot and dry that it burns your lungs as you take it in. Other than referring to it as "the place no sane person would want to spend any time," the best name for this most inhospitable environment truly is "the devastation." That's what the wilderness was in a literal sense for the people of Israel—a barren terrain hardly fit for life.

But as you read through the Bible, you discover that the term *wilderness* takes on a deeper meaning—a metaphorical, spiritual meaning. In the Scriptures, *wilderness* is used to describe a time in a person's life when his or her soul is parched and dry; when today is hard and the future appears barren; when as far as you can see there is nothing but devastation, and you wonder if you'll find a way out. Very often during that wilderness period, you feel all alone. You may even feel bereft of God's presence, as well.

One of my closest friends, a pastor named Brad, was diagnosed with colon cancer when he was forty-six. Soon it spread to his liver, and we were told that the disease most likely would be terminal. I often joked with Brad that even though we were the same age, he was who I wanted to be when I grew up. He was brilliant, full of compassion, and deeply spiritual. Brad knew God in a way few people do. His relationship with Christ was the center of his life—so much so that when I was in Brad's presence, I always felt that I was in the presence of God.

In the Scriptures,
wilderness is used to
describe a time in a person's life
when his or her soul is
parched and dry;
when today is hard and
the future appears barren;
when as far as you can see there is
nothing but devastation,
and you wonder if
you'll find a way out.

As the disease progressed, he once told me, "Robby, I don't understand. I'm old enough that I've actually learned how to do effective ministry. And I'm young enough that I still have the energy to work long and hard. At least I did before I got sick. All I ever wanted was to be a pastor. And now that I'm in my prime, it's being taken from me. I don't understand."

Brad confessed to me in an e-mail that for the first time in his life, he had a hard time praying. Before his cancer, he had prayed often and for long periods of time. But when he entered the wilderness of terminal cancer, his prayer life and his experience of God's presence changed.

He wrote, "I always saw prayer as a 'conversation.' I sensed that God was listening and responding to my prayers. Then, when I had cancer and needed that sensation, it wasn't there. I felt like I was talking out into the darkness and there wasn't even an echo. But I resolved to go on praying. I decided to pray the Lord's Prayer every night. That was all I could do, and I didn't feel God's presence when I did it."

There's more to Brad's story, which I'll share with you later. Before his death, prayer became fulfilling again, and the presence of God became real and sustaining to him. The way that he died, full of faith and comforting others who were suffering, was an example to me and to others just as the way that he lived had been. Yet while he was in the midst of the wilderness, he often had felt alone.

Brad's experience is common. When we are in the wilderness, those who are near us often do not seem to understand the depth of our pain and fear. And it may seem that God has abandoned us when we need him most.

When I have preached on the topic of the wilderness, I have encouraged church members to write to me about how they have felt during their wilderness experiences. Like Brad, people have written, "I was alone." Others have commented, "I was broken," "I was lost," "I was confused," "I was in pain," and "I was hopeless." One woman even echoed the meaning of the Hebrew word for wilderness, writing, "I was devastated."

In the wilderness you come to the end of yourself. There doesn't seem to be a way out, and you wonder if life will ever change. Without strength or hope, "Why go on?" is a question you ask yourself, waiting for an answer that never seems to come. You wonder if you ever will get through this terrible time and, if you do, if you will be better and stronger or beaten and broken.

The wilderness is that time when we learn the lessons that God has to teach us "old school"—that is, through suffering and persevering and trusting in a God whose plan we cannot comprehend and whose presence we may not feel. But there's no school like old school, and there's no place like the wilderness for growing in faith. In spite of its pain—actually, *because* of its pain—the wilderness is a place of great opportunity. It's where God can teach us life's most important lessons. As one of my friends told me after he went through the wilderness experience of losing his job, being unemployed for months, and battling cancer at the same time, "I wouldn't go through that again for a million dollars, but I wouldn't take all the money in the world for what I learned about walking with God."

Your wilderness will be the most difficult time in your life. But find the right way through your wilderness—God's way—and nothing will help you more to grow into a person of strength, character, and faith.

Who Can Expect to Spend Time in the Wilderness?

You, that's who. If you haven't already been through the wilderness, you will. And even if you have, chances are you'll have more wilderness experiences throughout your lifetime. At one time or another, everyone spends time in the wilderness.

When we search the Scriptures, we see that many of the people who spent time in the wilderness are the very people we find in Hebrews 11, often referred to as the "Faith Hall of Fame." Abraham, Sarah, Moses, David, and others walked through the wilderness long before their names were recorded in Hebrews 11. Even Jesus spent time in the wilderness.

Sometimes we American Christians seem to be more American than we are Christian. Often we think that following Jesus will make our lives easier and more successful—in terms of physical health and material prosperity. Some of our country's most popular preachers proclaim that living in faith will ensure that God will bless you with special treatment and favor—defining that shallowly as anything from getting a good parking space when shopping to experiencing financial abundance.

But God's purpose in our lives is not to make us happy. His Son died to make us holy. God's primary purpose in our lives is to make us more like Jesus. That's the best definition of holiness I know: being like Jesus. Making us more like his Son is also the greatest blessing God can give us. In order for us to be conformed to the image of Christ, we must suffer because he suffered. We must deny ourselves because he denied himself. We must care more about our character than our comfort because that's what we see in the life of our Lord. Instead of working to accumulate what this life offers, we must work on giving our lives away because that is what Jesus did. If we are to follow Christ and become more like him, we will have to spend some time in the wilderness because he spent time in the wilderness. (I will say more about that in just a moment.)

We have a tendency to believe that if we live right and follow Christ faithfully, we should not have to go through undeserved suffering and painful experiences. I have noticed that when life is especially difficult, people often feel singled out, as if God has specifically chosen them for unfair treatment. Often we want to know "Why me?" We demand an answer from God as to why *we* are being made to suffer and struggle. Sometimes the answer is simply "life is hard."

M. Scott Peck begins his modern classic *The Road Less Traveled* with these words: "Life is difficult."[2] He states that although we might know this truth intellectually, most of us rebel against the reality when we experience it ourselves. In so doing, we waste precious time and deplete our limited physical and emotional strength, which would be better spent learning the spiritual lessons that the problems of life can teach us.

Being a faithful follower of Jesus will not make life easier. In fact, in many ways, it makes life more difficult. Before giving our lives to Christ, we could accept the values of our culture and "conform to the pattern of this world" (Romans 12:2); in other words, we could live like everyone else. Before accepting Christ, we could pursue happiness as our highest priority and look to "the lust of the flesh, and the lust of the eyes, and the pride of life" (1 John 2:16) to find it. But now that we belong to Christ, we find ourselves fighting constantly against our sinful nature and a fallen world that would seduce us away from our Lord and Savior. This makes life hard—in some ways harder than when we felt we were free to do whatever we desired.

All of this is to say that when life is hard, you are not being singled out. Life is difficult for everyone. And the more serious you are about following Jesus, the more you will have to deny yourself and fight against the world and its temptations. Expect life to be hard. Expect that you will go through a wilderness—probably several before your life is over. It's part of the Christian life. In fact, it's a necessity if we are going to become more like Jesus.

When I was a freshman in college, Edward "Ted" Kennedy, Jr., was diagnosed with bone cancer. He was only twelve years old at the time. To save his life, his right leg was amputated. Cards, letters, phone calls, and telegrams came from all over the world to console him and his family. The Kennedys had suffered so much, including the assassination of two of Ted Jr.'s uncles, and the outpouring of love was overwhelming. Most of the messages carried similar sentiments of compassion and sympathy: "We are praying for you," "We love you," "Our hearts hurt for you." One, however, was very different. It came from a former Green Beret. He sent the boy his green beret along with a message intended to give him heart. In the message he included these simple and direct words: "It's a man's journey. Get on with it."[3]

Those may not be the words you or I would have sent, but they are important words for all of us to hear when we are in a wilderness. Life is hard, and it's hard for everyone. And those of us who have the idea that we will escape life's problems or that we are owed an explanation when we suffer pain and loss will fail to learn the lessons that the wilderness has to teach us. Life is not a child's game; it's a difficult journey. It won't go easy on any of us, and we shouldn't expect or want it to. Teddy Roosevelt wrote, "I have never in my life envied a human being who led an easy life; I have envied a great many people who led difficult lives and led them well."[4]

Ease and comfort do not create character and strength. A life without great challenges will not grow a great faith. Because we cannot be remade into the image of Jesus without trials and pain and loss, you can be sure that you will spend some time in the wilderness.

Why Does God Allow Us to Experience the Wilderness?

This is perhaps the most pervasive and unsettling question related to the wilderness experience. *Why* does God allow us to experience the wilderness?

God uses the wilderness to prepare his people. God uses the difficult, desperate times of our lives to teach us important lessons and develop our character, making us into the image of his Son, so that we will be ready for the future and equipped to be his instruments in a hurting and broken world.

The Father sent his Son to save the world and change the course of human history. Jesus came to create a new future for the broken and the lost. But before he began his ministry, he was led by the Spirit into the wilderness where he spent forty days fasting and being tempted. The Father knew that when Jesus began to preach the good news and set the captives free from the kingdom of darkness, he would be opposed by powerful men and attacked by the forces of hell. And before he would be able to declare, "It is finished," Jesus would have many battles to fight and win, both of the flesh and of the spirit. So, the Father sent his Son to that most difficult of places, the wilderness, where he was prepared for what was to come—it was part of the maturation process by which he "grew in wisdom and stature" (Luke 2:52) and through which he would learn to trust fully in the Father when he felt weak and tempted.

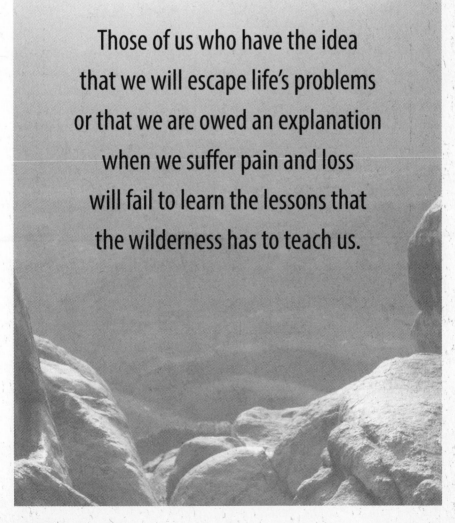

Those of us who have the idea
that we will escape life's problems
or that we are owed an explanation
when we suffer pain and loss
will fail to learn the lessons that
the wilderness has to teach us.

God is still doing his work of releasing the captives and saving the lost. That work is still being opposed by the powers of darkness, both human and demonic. Those who would join God in that work need to be faithful and strong just as Jesus was. Because the Father used the wilderness to prepare his Son for the life he was to live, we can be sure that he will use the wilderness to teach us the lessons that will strengthen our faith and refine our character.

It's in the wilderness that we learn not to trust our feelings but to depend on God's promises. It's there we experience that God's grace is sufficient and that even if we cannot see God at work, he is faithful to keep his word. Unlike any other time in our lives, the wilderness prepares us for difficult times ahead because it teaches us that God is faithful and trustworthy.

When I think about the preparation and teaching we undergo in the wilderness, I'm reminded of the four-wheel-drive truck commercials in which trucks are driven over the roughest terrain, making it look like the truck is about to be shaken apart. The announcer comes on and says, "This truck was tested in the proving grounds of the Baja," or some other rugged and remote place. Then the scene changes. The truck cruises into a suburban driveway, and the keys are given to a guy in khakis and loafers. The point: "We've put this truck through more than you'll ever ask it to do. And it came through just fine. It's tested. Proven. It's ready for whatever you have in mind."

That's how God uses the wilderness in our lives. It becomes a proving ground so that once we get through it, we can look life square in the face and say, "Do what you want. I've been through tough times. I've learned to walk with God, and I know how to walk in faith. I'm not afraid because I've learned that God and I can get through anything together. And I'm ready to be used for his purposes."

What, specifically, is God preparing us for in the wilderness? I believe there are two answers to this question.

1. The Wilderness Prepares Us for Blessing

One of the great truths Jesus taught is that God loves us and wants to bless us even more than we love and want to bless our own children. Comparing God to us and our willingness to give our children the good things they desire, Jesus said, "How much more will your Father in heaven give good gifts to those who ask him!" (Matthew 7:11).

But wise parents know that not every child is ready for every gift. What would benefit a child when he or she has matured can be destructive if the child receives the gift too early in life. That's why wills and trusts often stipulate that a child must be a certain age or meet a certain goal, such as graduating from college, before receiving what the parent ultimately wants the child to have. The parent knows that if a child is lacking in maturity and character, receiving what is meant to be a blessing might actually destroy that child's life.

Winning thousands or millions of dollars in a state-sponsored lottery would seem like a formula for lifelong happiness. But it does just the opposite for many people. In fact, people who win larger amounts are more likely to go bankrupt than those who win smaller amounts.[5] The "blessing" of sudden wealth often creates more problems than it solves for persons who lack wisdom, discipline, and humility.

Any blessing can become a curse if the one who receives the gift does not have the character to bear the blessing—be it finances, recognition, influence, or even marriage and children. So before God blesses us, often he allows us to go through a wilderness experience that humbles our spirit and refines our character. Then we have the maturity that can bear the blessing.

When Moses led the Israelites out of bondage in Egypt, they marched through the wilderness and came to the Promised Land. God told them to go into the land and take it. But they refused. They were afraid of the tribes who lived there, and they acted in fear rather than faith.

God sent them back into the wilderness where they wandered for the next forty years. When they were ready, God brought them back to the Promised Land. He told them, "This is the land I promised to your ancestors. It's a land of abundance." He went into great detail, telling them that they would be blessed with much grain and wine and oil. Their herds would prosper. They would come to possess gold and silver and iron. But he also reminded them about the wilderness that preceded this time of blessing:

> *Remember the long way that the* LORD *your God has led you these forty years in the wilderness, in order to humble you, testing you to know what was in your heart, whether or not you would keep his commandments. He humbled you by letting you hunger, then by feeding you with manna, with which neither you nor your ancestors were acquainted, in order to make you understand that one does not live by bread alone, but by every word that comes from the mouth of the* LORD. *(Deuteronomy 8:2-3 NRSV)*

The wilderness period was meant to humble the Israelites and create within them the character that could bear the blessing God had for them. That too is one of the purposes of the wilderness experiences in our lives. God will use the wilderness to humble us. God wants to teach us to trust in him, not in what we possess. He wants us to come to the end ourselves so that we will look to him as our Source and our Savior. It's in our times of brokenness and despair, when our wisdom is insufficient and our strength proves inadequate, that we are humbled. It's in the wilderness, when our lives make no sense and the illusion that we are in control is taken from us, that we learn to depend on God. And if we are truly humbled, we learn how to walk with him when we have nothing so we will remember to walk faithfully with him later when we are blessed with much.

It's in the wilderness we learn to trust in the Provider, not in the provision. It's in the times when we have nothing that we learn to depend upon the Giver, not the gift. It's when all we have to hold onto is God and his promises that we discover God and his promises are enough.

Unless we have been tested and proven, it's very likely that an abundance of blessing will warp our values and steal our hearts from the God who has blessed us. Without realizing it, we will turn our eyes to what we possess and love the life we have, instead of looking to the Giver and loving him with all we are. In the wilderness we are prepared for blessing. It teaches us to hold on to the Blesser tightly so that later we will hold on to our blessings loosely.

2. The Wilderness Prepares Us for Battle

Another way God uses the wilderness is to prepare us for battle. When God brought the Israelites back to the Promised Land, he basically said, "There are seven tribes in the land that are bigger than you. Taking the land will be a battle. But you're ready now. Act in faith. Do not give in to fear, and the land will be yours."

If you want the life of blessing that God has for you, you too will have battles to fight—for yourself and for others. Jesus promised us, "In this world you will have trouble" (John 16:33). We can count on it. If we are going to be faithful to God, we will have to battle against adversity. We will have battles with temptation. We will have to fight against materialism and self-centeredness. We will have to fight against discouragement. We will have to defeat the lies of the world. There are battles we all must fight and win to walk with God and do his will.

There is a big story going on around us. A cosmic war is being fought: God is at work in the world to find the lost, release the prisoners, and bring them out of the kingdom of darkness and death into his kingdom of light and life. If you decide that you want to be part of this big story, then you are signing up for a life that will battle against the evil, the injustice, and the darkness in your own life and in the lives of others. God wants to use you to minister to the needs and wounds of men and women, wounds that threaten to keep them from experiencing his grace. God wants you to use what you learn in the wilderness not only for your sake but also for the sake of others.

I hope that's the life you choose. It's impossible to be a faithful follower of Jesus and choose any other life. But in choosing this life, you will have spiritual battles to fight that will require courage and faith and suffering and perseverance. The wilderness is where our character is formed and we learn that God can be trusted even when we cannot see how the battle will be won. The wilderness is where we learn to be obedient when obedience doesn't seem to make sense.

The wilderness is where we learn to walk by faith, not by sight, because often in the wilderness everything we see makes our cause seem hopeless and our efforts seem futile.

In many great books and inspiring movies there is an all-important battle that must be won. If the world is to be made right, if evil is to be defeated, and if captives are to be freed, there is a moment when the forces of good must defeat the armies of evil. But before that final battle is fought, there is always a prior battle that must be won. The hero must first win the war within his or her own heart. Some commitment must be made. Some fear must be faced. Some lie must be rejected. Some risk must be taken. Some sacrifice must be made. Some temptation must be overcome. Some truth must be claimed.

In every great life, great battles must be fought and won. And the most important battle is always fought and won in the heart of the hero. But it must be *fought*. We must go through the wilderness because it is there that the battles of the heart are so often won. It's where God trains and prepares us to fight his battles that change us and later change the world.

Virginia was in her sixties when I knew her. She was very thin and frail, like a little bird. I never saw her without a beautiful smile on her face and a mischievous twinkle in her eyes. Virginia had Parkinson's disease. When I knew her, she shook all the time. Sometimes the shaking would increase as I was talking to her, and I'd have to reach out and grab her and settle her down a bit.

Virginia had a great heart in every way. Our church was young at the time, and so was our community. Virginia was one of our few older members. But what an example she was to the rest of us, being faithful in worship every Sunday and always having an encouraging spirit. When we announced that we were starting a ministry to aid poor families in our community, Virginia came to the first meeting and all the ones that followed. She was a part of everything we did to help needy people—shaking and smiling all the while—simply because she cared about others. It was in her heart to love and help and serve. She was so full of joy in all she did. Knowing how difficult her disease had made her life, it was hard to comprehend how she could be so content.

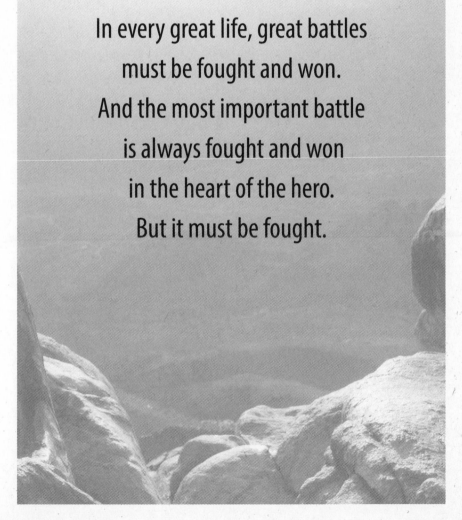

In every great life, great battles
must be fought and won.
And the most important battle
is always fought and won
in the heart of the hero.
But it must be fought.

Another trait I admired was her adventurous nature. She and another woman, almost as old as Virginia, teamed up and went everywhere together. "Road trip" was their favorite phrase. (I thought of them as an elderly version of Thelma and Louise.) One of their favorite things to do was to throw their fishing poles into the back of the car, drive ninety miles to Galveston, and spend the whole day fishing. It frightened me to think about little Virginia shaking and driving, barely able to see over the steering wheel.

Virginia always loved the water and took a swimming class at the community athletic center. One of her friends told me this story:

> You'll never believe what Virginia did. Swimming class was over and we were all getting out of the water and drying off. But we didn't see Virginia. "Where is she?" someone asked. "Oh, my goodness," we heard someone else shriek. Virginia was standing on the edge of the high diving board, shaking. No sooner did I cry out, "Virginia, don't," than she dove off like it was nothing. When we pulled her out, I scolded her: "Virginia, what were you doing?" She said, "I just wanted to see if I could do it or not."

People like Virginia have always intrigued me. They face their problems head on, live with joy, and serve others even when their own life is hard. So one day I asked Virginia, "How did you become you? I mean, how did you get this heart that's in you? You're not afraid of anything." And she told me a story.

Her husband had worked for a family-owned company. Given the nature of the business, he was on call 24/7, often leaving home at all hours of the day or night whenever there was a problem. When the owner died, there was a family dispute over the company, and Virginia's husband was a casualty. Each of the owner's children thought he might be loyal to the other, so they solved the problem by firing him. He was dismissed without any kind of severance package or any appreciation for all the sacrifices he had made. The blow was so devastating that he put a gun to his head and killed himself. He left a note asking Virginia to forgive him for being a failure.

Virginia found herself with close to nothing financially, a job that paid very little, three children she cared about dearly, a thousand questions, and a broken heart. Already diagnosed with Parkinson's, the future looked dark for Virginia. At times she was anxious and afraid. At other times she struggled with anger and bitterness. She lived with these emotions all the time, with them continually building within her.

Absolutely overwrought one day, Virginia drove out to a big lake near her house. Water always had been a kind of therapy for her. She dove in and began to swim as fast and as far as she could. She finally stopped when she was so exhausted that she couldn't swim another stroke. When she turned around and saw how far from shore she was, she realized she would never be able to swim back. She began to scream, but there was no one there to hear.

She described what happened:

> I panicked and I began to thrash about. I went under, and I came back up. I yelled for help. I went back under. And when I managed to get to the surface, I knew that if I went down again, I'd never come back up. Then a voice spoke to me. It was God's voice. And God's voice said, "Virginia, if you keep fighting and thrashing about, you're going to go under and you'll die. Take a breath. Relax. Lean back, and let me hold you up." And I did. And he did.
>
> I've learned that whenever I get anxious, whenever I feel like there's not an answer inside of me that can handle what I'm facing, if I will just look to God, remember his love for me, and lean back, he'll hold me up. And I've never had to be afraid again.

The wilderness humbled Virginia. Being alone with no skills to speak of, a future that seemed hopeless, and no idea how to solve her problems brought her to the end of herself. It didn't make her weak. I don't think I've ever known a stronger woman. But it taught her to find her strength in God. She came to know what the Apostle Paul discovered, that God's power is made perfect in our weakness; for when we acknowledge our weakness, then we are strong (see 2 Corinthians 12:9-10). With the lessons she learned and the strength she gained through her time in the wilderness, Virginia fought and won several battles. She overcame anxiety and anger. She maintained an adventurous spirit despite a debilitating illness. She lived a Christ-centered life that served others when it would have been so easy to be consumed with her own problems. The lessons she learned in the wilderness of losing her husband prepared her for many battles to come.

Like Virginia, God wants to bless you and use you to fight his battles in the world—battles that will make you strong and enable you to bring life, healing, and hope into the lives of others. Receiving those blessings and fighting those battles will require the character and strength that come from a faith forged in the hot desert air of the wilderness. Don't see your time there as a sign that life is being unfair to you or that God has forgotten you. Just the opposite is true. God uses the wilderness to prepare you for a future of blessing and for battles that will achieve his good purposes for you and for many others. Learn the lessons he has to teach you, hard as they may be. And remember: whatever sacrifices you must make to go through the wilderness, God's way will be well worth it.

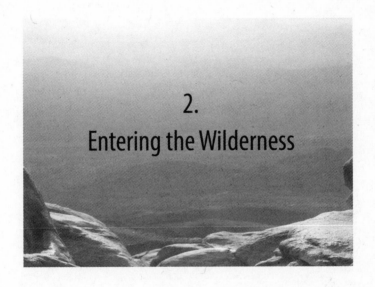

2.
Entering the Wilderness

2.
Entering the Wilderness

We've seen that the wilderness is a barren time of devastation that God can use to prepare us for blessing and battle. And we've acknowledged that the wilderness is no respecter of persons. It is something that every one of us will experience along life's journey, regardless of how we have lived our lives. In the Scriptures we find that people entered the wilderness when they were unfaithful as well as when they were faithful. The Israelites spent forty years in the wilderness because they were disobedient when God told them to enter the Promised Land, yet Jesus also was led into the wilderness when he had been nothing but faithful.

Immediately before he was driven into the wilderness, Jesus was baptized by John the Baptist, and the Spirit of God came in the form of a dove and rested on him. The Father reached out of heaven and, by his Spirit, put his hand on his Son's shoulder and announced from heaven, "This is my Son, whom I love; with him I am well pleased" (Matthew 3:17). The Father essentially said to the Son, "I've been watching you, and everything you have done has pleased me. Every step you have taken has been right. I am delighted in who you are. Your life brings me great joy. I love you, Son. Now, it's time to go to the wilderness."

From our human perspective, this does not make sense. Though we might understand why the disobedient Israelites were sent to wander in the wilderness for forty years, we have difficulty comprehending why someone who is faithful has to spend time there. In addition to Jesus, the Bible gives us many other examples of individuals who entered the wilderness despite their obedience in doing God's will.

Consider the prophet Elijah. His wilderness experience came immediately after he had faithfully and courageously done all that God had asked him to do. For years he had given his life to bringing the Israelites back to God, praying for them, and even risking his life for them. His heart had longed to see the day that they would reject the pagan god Baal and return to the God of Abraham, Isaac, and Jacob. Finally the day came. He and the prophets of Baal agreed that the god who sent fire down from heaven to consume their sacrifice would be proclaimed the one true God.

For hours the prophets of Baal implored their god with their prayers, dancing, and shouting, but nothing happened. Finally they began slashing themselves with their swords, thinking that the sight of their blood would move Baal to act. Still nothing. The Bible says that Elijah began taunting the false prophets: "'Shout louder!' he said. 'Surely he is a god! Perhaps he is deep in thought, or busy, or traveling. Maybe he is sleeping and must be awakened'" (1 Kings 18:27). Finally, the prophets of Baal gave up.

Elijah stepped forward, offered his sacrifice, and prayed; and immediately God sent fire and consumed the offering and the altar. The moment Elijah had dreamed of, prayed for, and risked his life for had come to be. "When all the people saw this, they fell prostrate and cried, 'The LORD—he is God! The LORD—he is God!'" (1 Kings 18:39). The prophets of Baal were destroyed, and the people of Israel proclaimed Yahweh as God.

There are many great moments in the Old Testament, but you'd be hard pressed to find one that is more dramatic than Elijah's victory over the false god Baal. Imagine how Elijah must have felt. His work, his faithfulness, and his willingness to risk his life had won a great victory for God. God had proven himself sovereign and had used Elijah to bring his people back to himself. Talk about as good as it gets! Yet, in the very next chapter, we find Elijah in the wilderness, depressed and asking God to take his life. We human beings are complicated creatures!

Years ago I read a cartoon in which a little figure who appeared to be overwhelmed and depressed said, "In my next life I want to come back as something easier than a human being." The truth is that we get only one life, and it's not easy for any of us. Being biological creatures, our emotions tend to go up and down. Being sinful in nature, we tend to make life about us and our needs. Being self-absorbed, we tend to face the challenges of life on our own when there are others around us who are willing to help. Even the best of us can be on top of the world one day only to find ourselves face down in the wilderness the next, having forgotten all the ways that God has proven his faithfulness to us in the past.

I wish I could give you a formula for avoiding the wilderness: do this and you will never spend time in the wilderness. But that's not the way that life works. There's no predicting exactly when you might enter the wilderness; there's only the certainty that you will. There are, however, some common pathways that lead into the wilderness—some ways that people often enter the wilderness. Let's look at four different entry points.

1. Our Own Decisions and Actions

Sometimes we end up in a wilderness through our own bad decisions and wrong actions.

Recall the children of Israel. After four hundred years of bondage, God used Moses to deliver them from slavery. They rushed out of Egypt and, in a relatively short time, came to the Promised Land. God said to them, "There's the land I have prepared for you. It's a good land, full of blessing. Go in and take it; it's yours." But the people of Israel said, "Not so fast, God. We sent some spies to check things out, and they reported that there are other tribes living in the land who are strong and whose cities are fortified. They'll destroy us if we go in." God persisted, "Trust me. I will go before you. I will fight your battles. This is your land. I'm giving it to you. Go in, follow me, and take it." But instead of being faithful to God's command and acting in faith, they gave in to their fear. They turned around, and for the next forty years they wandered in the wilderness.

Sometimes that's how our wilderness begins, too. We choose our way instead of God's way. We make moral mistakes. We're unfaithful in our marriage, we act unethically at work, or we wrongly handle the stress of life by turning to alcohol or drugs or something else that is equally harmful to us. Instead of turning to God and facing life's challenges with integrity and courage, we choose something or someone else in hopes of easing the pressure and pain.

People often have affairs because they are unsatisfied in their marriages. Repairing a failing marriage is hard work. It requires becoming vulnerable by admitting our hurt, acknowledging our part in the marriage's decline, forgiving another person, and learning new ways of communicating. Many seem to believe that an easier option is seeking the affirmation and gratification that come from sexual experiences with another person outside the marriage. So they enjoy the pleasure of physical intimacy with someone they can simply walk away from when he or she is no longer pleasing. I will never forget the man who told me many years ago, "I had lost all feeling for my wife, my children, and my work. I was dead inside. I had an affair to see if I could feel anything at all." What he felt very soon was the devastation that came when he broke the heart of a woman who loved him and lost the respect of a son who admired him.

A young woman in her early twenties came to see me one day. She had flunked out of college. Making passing grades and doing heroin had proven to be difficult to pull off at the same time. I asked how she started using heroin. She told me, "I always felt awkward around others, especially in groups. In high school, I started drinking at parties. And then it was pills. In college, I needed something more to feel okay about myself. Eventually, it took a needle in my arm."

The teenage years of not fitting in and feeling like no one would like the real you can be a terrible wilderness of self-doubt and pain. Many of us were tempted to find a way to change how we felt and make it easier to fit in. But removing the pain without addressing the problem is never the way of growth, health, or long-term happiness. Often it's the way of emotional, spiritual, and sometimes physical death.

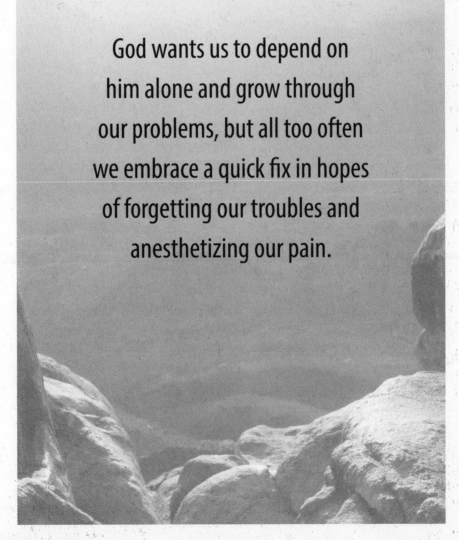

God wants us to depend on
him alone and grow through
our problems, but all too often
we embrace a quick fix in hopes
of forgetting our troubles and
anesthetizing our pain.

God wants us to depend on him alone and grow through our problems, but all too often we embrace a quick fix in hopes of forgetting our troubles and anesthetizing our pain. That's how so many of our self-destructive mistakes originate. Instead of facing the unpleasant realities of our lives with God-given strength and discipline, we try to sedate our anxiety and fears with a drink, a drug, an exciting (and often illicit) relationship, or greater material or professional success. Later we realize that what promised immediate peace and comfort did nothing but take us to a place of devastation. What we hoped would bring life created barrenness and destruction for us—and often for those we love.

2. The Actions of Others

Just as there are times when we enter the wilderness because of our own mistakes and choices, there also are times when we enter the wilderness because of the actions of others.

We began this chapter with a brief glimpse of Elijah, who was a faithful prophet and a man of great strength during one of Israel's most difficult periods. King Ahab and Queen Jezebel had built a temple to Baal in Samaria, had encouraged false prophets, and had the prophets of Yahweh put to death. For years Elijah had stood firm and had called the people of Israel back to God.

Like an Old Testament version of the classic movie *Gunfight at the O.K. Corral*, Elijah faced off against the prophets of Baal and won a great victory that clearly demonstrated that Yahweh is God. When Jezebel heard what had happened, she sent a messenger to Elijah with her promise that she would put him to death or die trying. Elijah was gripped with fear and fled into the wilderness to hide from Jezebel. Because of Jezebel's threat, in only a matter of hours this strong man of faith was not only in the wilderness, the wilderness was in him. We read, "He himself went farther on into the desert a day's journey. He finally sat down under a solitary broom bush. He longed for his own death: 'It's more than enough, Lord! Take my life because I'm no better than my ancestors'" (1 Kings 19:4 CEB).

Both emotionally and spiritually, Elijah was absolutely empty. Overcome with a sense of hopelessness and despair, he prayed, "God, I can't do this anymore. I'm at the end of myself. Just let me die." When God asked what he was doing in the wilderness, he responded, "I alone am left" (1 Kings 19:10 NRSV). That's the way it often feels in the wilderness. We feel alone with the weight of the world on our shoulders, and it's more than we can bear. Of course, Elijah wasn't alone. God told him that there were seven thousand others who had not bowed the knee to Baal (see 1 Kings 19:18). We always feel more alone in the wilderness than we really are. Nevertheless, Jezebel's death threat was very real, and it drove him into the wilderness.

Like Elijah, sometimes we end up in the wilderness because the actions of others have brought us pain and devastation. When people have told me about their wilderness experiences, they often have talked about the actions of others—a spouse who had an affair, a business partner who betrayed them, or a child who became addicted to alcohol or drugs. Regardless of the differing circumstances, all have described the fear, helplessness, and false guilt that the other person's actions have caused them to experience.

One woman wrote to me about her daughter who was diagnosed with bipolar disorder. She said that she had tried desperately to get her daughter to take her medication but with little success. She described how utterly devastating it was to watch her daughter make one mistake after another, all the while trying to love her child in a way that would draw her back to God and bring her healing.

When you love someone, you allow yourself to become vulnerable. People will tell you that the "right" response is to set boundaries and separate your own well-being from the well-being of the person you love. They'll advise you not to make your happiness dependent on his or her behavior. Ultimately, that is the right thing to do. But when it's your child or spouse who is on drugs or in prison or suffering with mental illness, properly detaching from this person you care about so deeply is extremely difficult. It feels as if you've given up, as if you're being disloyal and failing to do what a caring parent or spouse should do. When you love someone whose life is out of control and who will not accept your help or the help of others, you are likely to find yourself confused, hurting, and hopeless.

The flip side is when someone who is supposed to love you is uncaring, disloyal, or even brutal. In a church I once served, there was a couple who were in their eighties and were always together, showing each other great kindness and compassion. So I was very surprised when Frances came to the church and, showing no sign of sorrow, told me that Jim had died in the night at home. In fact, she almost seemed happy. It just didn't make sense. I expressed concern for her and asked a few questions, and finally she said something that explained why she was not grieving as I had expected: "I'm so happy for him. It's over now."

"What's that, Frances?" I asked.

"All his suffering and unhappiness," she responded.

When I asked her to explain, this is what she said: "His father was a brutal man, and Jim was never able to escape the abuse he suffered. He often woke up screaming and sweating in the middle of the night. Just last week, I heard him crying in bed next to me. I put my arms around him and placed his head back on the pillow. He whispered to me, 'Oh those beatings, I can feel them still.'" The actions of one who should have loved and protected him put Jim in a wilderness of pain where he lived all his life.

When we are hurt deeply and unfairly, we need to acknowledge that pain and grieve. In fact, it's okay to be angry. Anger in the face of injustice and brutality is both a right and healthy response, even when we are the ones who have been made to suffer. However, there is a right way to handle our hurt and anger. After acknowledging it fully and feeling the depth of our pain, we need to bring it to God and ask him to cleanse us of the venom it has left in our souls. We can pray that God will give us the grace to forgive those who have hurt us, and as he works in our lives, we can become emotionally and spiritually healthy again.

Unfortunately, too often we hold on to our anger, and it leads to bitterness. Like poison that is swallowed, it begins to destroy us from the inside out. As a result, our spirits become like a wasteland. We dry up inside, no longer able to enjoy the blessings of life or the goodness of God. For some of us, the injustice we suffer is a spouse's betrayal, the disloyalty of a friend, or some form of physical or emotional abuse. For others, like Jim, the wound came early in life from a parent who was cruel or absent. However we receive them, deep wounds can create a wilderness within us if we do not release them to God. Often we wind up wandering through life in pain, feeling far from God.

Every year I lead a small-group experience for men called "Making Peace with Your Past."[1] Even though I have led groups for fifteen years, I am always amazed when a new group of men muster the courage to open up and tell others about the pain of their childhoods—the words that cursed them, the brutality that broke their spirits, or the demeaning of their gifts and dreams that took their hearts from them. Because I am familiar with the seriousness and depth of pain that many people live with for decades, please know that I say this with the utmost sensitivity and gentleness: you may have entered a wilderness because of what has been done to you, but you remain there because of the choices you make. I say this not as a word of condemnation but as a word of hope. You see, there is a way out of your wilderness, as we will explore in the chapters to follow. Holding on to your hurt is understandable. Having a hard time forgiving your offender is to be expected. And often we need the help of a pastor or a counselor to find healing and let go of our pain. But giving in to bitterness and refusing to let it go is your decision. And it is a mistake that will keep you in the wilderness for as long as you allow it.

3. The Natural Flow of Life

We can enter the wilderness through our own bad choices and mistakes or those that others have made, but sometimes there's not anything that anyone has done to cause our wilderness experience. Sometimes we enter the wilderness simply because of the natural flow of life.

In the Old Testament, Abraham and Sarah were living a normal life when God called them to follow him to a new land, and their journey took them through the wilderness. In the natural flow of living obediently to God, they found themselves in the wilderness—

literally as well as experientially. In the New Testament, we read that Jesus encountered many who were experiencing great trials due to the natural flow of life. There were people who were sick and in need of healing, such as the woman with the issue of blood, as well as those who were grieving the loss of a loved one, such as Mary and Martha after the death of their brother, Lazarus. Even Jesus himself was overcome with grief after the loss of his dear friend Lazarus.

We can relate to the devastation that can come from the natural flow of life. Our company downsizes, we are let go, and our lives become a wilderness. We wonder, *Who am I? Where do I go? God, why is this happening?* Or perhaps a loved one becomes seriously ill, and we're so consumed with caring for their needs and worrying about what will happen that we become empty and dry. Other times we lose someone close to us. One man told me that within an eight-year-period he lost six close family members and that it had ripped his heart out. He lived with a constant sense of loss. Like an angry sea, every time he felt he could gain his footing and stand, another wave of grief came crashing down upon him. There was no one to blame. No one was at fault, but still he struggled with himself and with God. He prayed, "God, I don't understand. Why is this happening? Why my family? Don't you know? Don't you care?"

There also are transition periods of life that can send us into the wilderness. For some of us, the teenage years are a wilderness. For many of us—including skinny, pencil-necked kids like me—those are hard, desolate years. Everyone else seems to be happy and "together," yet we spend those years asking, *Where do I fit in? Will anyone ever love me? Will I ever find a place where it feels right to be me?* As we later discovered, it did get better. God had better days ahead for us. Eventually we came out of that wilderness and were amazed at who we had become. Other transition periods can bring a similar wilderness experience, such as when we are adjusting to getting married, having children, or entering into a new stage or phase of life.

The natural flow of life brings
periods of transition and change.
Each transition period is like a
death. . . . As with every death,
it is natural to mourn and grieve.
But it's better to see these
transition periods as opportunities
for a new birth.

Some moms enter a wilderness when their children leave home. They love their kids with all their hearts. They invest their lives in preparing their children for the future. They do their job so well that their kids grow up, become independent, and move out. They have every reason to celebrate a job well done, except now they have a huge hole in their heart. They poured their lives into their children, and now they're gone. That can be devastating. Often as a child moves out, a wilderness period moves in, and mothers can find themselves wondering, *Who am I now? Where do I share all this love that I have to give?* It's especially hard when the child doesn't seem to appreciate what he or she was given. An empty nest can easily turn into an empty and broken heart.

A natural transition that can create a wilderness for men is middle age. They come to the place where they have everything the world has told them they need in order to be happy, but they're not. They finally slow down enough to look within, and they discover that their souls are empty. They're no longer that twenty-something who said, "I'm going to be a success and make a name for myself." They're now forty or fifty years old and established in life, but there is a sadness within that has come with the realization that the treasures, toys, praises, and pleasures of this world are not enough to fill the longings within a man's heart. For many men, this is a time of real confusion and pain. They find themselves full of regret and loss. Some realize they have sacrificed their families and their souls for things that can never satisfy the deepest desires within them. And if not that dramatic, their realization is that they gave the first half of their lives to priorities fit for a boy but not a man. This period of transition holds great promise for men who will use it to connect deeply with the God who "has placed eternity in their hearts" (Ecclesiastes 3:11). But in order to find the answers that will make them whole, they often must pass through a wilderness of self-examination and painful remorse.

The natural flow of life brings periods of transition and change. Each transition period is like a death. We find ourselves saying good-bye to the life we have known and maybe to the plans we have made. As with every death, it is natural to mourn and grieve. But it's better to see these transition periods as opportunities for a new birth.

Yes, there will be labor pangs, but the changes that occur around us, wanted or unwanted, are pregnant with the possibility of a new and better life. We can fight against them or we can embrace them. One will keep us in the wilderness; the other will lead us to a better place. This brings us to a fourth and final entry point into the wilderness.

4. The Plan of God

Sometimes—and please hear the emphasis on *sometimes*—a wilderness experience can be God's plan for us. There are times when a specific purpose of God requires us to go through difficult periods of trial, struggle, and suffering.

We need to be very careful here. God doesn't choose for us to suffer in an abusive marriage. God doesn't will for children to get cancer. God doesn't cause automobile accidents that injure our loved ones or take them from us. All of those experiences may bring a wilderness into our lives, but those are not the wilderness experiences that God wills for us.

What I have in mind are times that are spiritually dry and difficult. We continue to pray but our circumstances don't change—the job we thought we were going to get doesn't come through; we ask God for a friend or for a spouse and still we are alone; we long for a purpose that will give our lives meaning but we continue to feel dead inside. These are times when our faith is tested and we cannot understand why God doesn't act to answer our prayers. Almost all of the great saints went through an experience that is referred to as "the dark night of the soul," a time when God seemed far away and they wondered what he was doing in their lives. And what they report is that in these times God was able to teach them to trust him and his promises, not their feelings or their ability to understand what he was doing in their lives. Sometimes it is God's plan for us to experience a difficult time for the very same reason.

This concept is not popular in today's Americanized Christian environment. The most popular preachers on television proclaim that God's primary purpose in the universe is to make certain that your life is easy, comfortable, and prosperous. Appealing to our self-centeredness and our fallen desire to be the center of the universe, they present God as a cosmic valet who exists to make certain we get everything we want out of life and are never inconvenienced or bothered by the difficulties that other people endure.

When we read the Bible, we discover that God's plan for us is much better than we could ever imagine, but it does involve pain, struggle, and suffering. As we explored in the previous chapter, God wants to remake us into the image of Christ. That is his great goal for us. And we don't develop the character of Christ without pain, struggle, and suffering. That's why James told his readers: "Consider it pure joy, my brothers and sisters, whenever you face trials of many kinds, because you know that the testing of your faith produces perseverance. Let perseverance finish its work so that you may be mature and complete, not lacking anything" (James 1:2-4).

Consider Simon Peter, the disciple God would use to lead the other apostles after the death and resurrection of Jesus. The night before his crucifixion, Jesus said to Peter, "Simon, Simon, Satan has asked to sift you as wheat. But I have prayed for you" (Luke 22:31). What did Jesus pray? That he would not be tempted or tested? That he would not go through a difficult time? No, Jesus said, "I have prayed for you that your faith won't fail" (22:32a CEB). With these words I believe Jesus was telling Peter that God was going to allow him to be tested for a reason—so that his faith could be proven and he could be prepared for the work that he must do after Jesus was gone. In the same verse, Jesus continued, "When you have returned, strengthen your brothers and sisters" (22:32b CEB). He was essentially saying to Peter, "I've prayed for you. It's going to be hard, and you're going to make mistakes. But you'll come back, and you'll be stronger than ever. I will help you. But this time of testing is in keeping with the Father's will."

Just as Jesus said he would, Peter failed to be faithful. He denied Jesus, and his life became a wilderness. But later Jesus restored and commissioned Peter when he said to him, "Feed my sheep" (John 21:17). Peter's wilderness experience so re-formed him that shortly thereafter he preached boldly before thousands on the Day of Pentecost; he defied the Jewish authorities who told him to stop preaching, telling them, "We must obey God rather than any human authority" (Acts 5:29 NRSV); and he never again denied Jesus, even when being faithful required his own death.

In the Gospel of Matthew, we see God himself leading his own Son into the wilderness. We read, "Then the Spirit led Jesus up into the wilderness so that the devil might tempt him" (Matthew 4:1 CEB). The Spirit of God led Jesus into the wilderness for a period of testing and tempting so that he would be ready for all that was to come. It was only after this wilderness experience that Jesus began his public ministry.

What do you want in a pastor? A good preacher? A competent administrator? Someone with good people skills? People will often say about a pastor, "He's so gifted" or "She's so talented." All of those traits can be helpful. But what I want is someone who has been broken. Until a man or woman has been humbled, until a pastor has come to the end of himself or herself, that pastor's ministry will be built on his or her strengths rather than on the grace and power of God.

One of the great privileges of my life was serving on the staff of First United Methodist Church in downtown Houston where Bill Hinson was the senior pastor. Bill was a man of immense strength and courage. I have never known anyone who was more principled or had more integrity. When he spoke, I was always convicted that I needed to give more of myself to God and become more like Jesus.

I served with Bill the three years before he retired. Our annual reviews were—well, interesting. He always told me exactly how I needed to change and improve. But he would always end by looking me in the eyes and saying, "Rob, I love you." And I knew he did. When I told others who had served with Bill in previous years about this, some would look at me, surprised, and simply say, "Well, Bill has changed."

When Bill first came to First Church, it was facing difficult times. The oil industry was going through a bust and the crime rate in Houston was high. As soon as the workday ended, people seemed to leave downtown Houston as quickly as they could. Getting them to come back downtown on a Sunday was difficult to say the least.

Many of the members had moved their membership to suburban churches closer to where they lived. Attendance was down, finances were weak, the building was in disrepair, and morale was low.

For most of his years in ministry, Bill had been sent to churches that were struggling. He would work hard—often seventy hours a week—to turn a church around. Once it became strong, he would be sent to another church that was going through a hard time, and the process would begin all over again.

So, in some ways, First Church and its problems were a good fit for Bill. By the time he retired, not only was the downtown church doing well, Bill had led the congregation to start a large second campus with a two-thousand-seat sanctuary on the growing, west side of Houston. But I knew what it had cost him.

I think one of his finest moments came at a conference when pastors from all over the country had come to hear about the success story of an old downtown church that had found new life. As Bill told these young pastors about all that the church had accomplished, I could see the admiration in their eyes. They were hanging on to his every word and soaking up every lesson he had to teach. I could tell they were feeling the same way I had felt so many times—they wanted to be like him. Forget Michael Jordan, we wanted to be like Bill. And then in a beautiful act of vulnerability, Bill gave those young pastors a marvelous gift. He opened his heart and told them about his lowest moment.

Bill had never faced a situation he couldn't handle. No matter how bad off it was when he got there, he would put that church on his back, he said—put his shoulder to the grindstone and not stop working until it was strong and healthy. Tired, sick, it didn't matter. He would do it! And he did. Every time.

Until he got to Houston. No matter what he did, he couldn't turn the church around. Nothing he had done before worked. Nothing new he tried made a difference. It was the biggest challenge of his life, and he felt like he was failing. For the first time in his life, he wasn't strong enough to do what he believed God wanted him to do.

Bill became depressed. He couldn't sleep. He lost weight. The joy of ministry and life were disappearing. A doctor in the church recommended that he see a counselor, which he did.

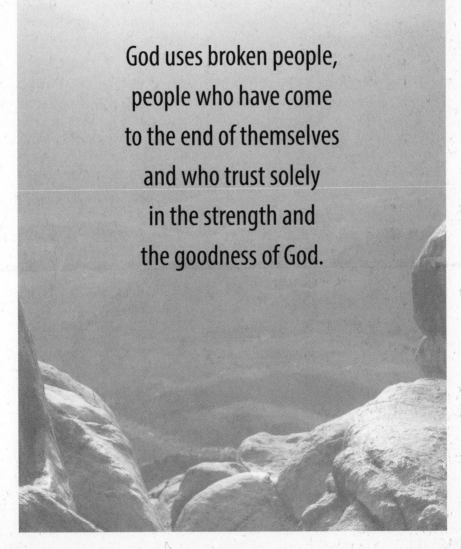

God uses broken people,
people who have come
to the end of themselves
and who trust solely
in the strength and
the goodness of God.

One Sunday after church was over and everyone had left, Bill knelt down at the altar in that beautiful sanctuary and prayed, "I can't do this anymore, God. I give up. This isn't my church anymore. It's your church. I'm sorry I ever acted like it was mine. You carry it; I can't. If it's going to succeed, you'll have to make it succeed. Do with me whatever you want. I am yours. Do with this church whatever you desire. It's yours."

Not only did the church grow and become strong and vibrant again, but Bill's heart was changed. His preaching became more characterized by compassion. He found a new ability to be with people and to love people. Before he came to the end of himself, what he had told me often—"I love you"—he had almost never spoken to staff members. Preparing for a talk I was to give a year later about what staff admire in a visionary leader, I surveyed the staff at First Church and asked them what they admired most in Bill. It wasn't his strength or his vision or his courage. Almost everyone said, "He loves me and he cares about my family."

Bill's last years were his best years. Why? Because of time spent in the wilderness. There he came to the end of his own strength so that he could learn to minister fully in the strength of God.

We want gifted pastors and spiritual leaders, but God uses broken people, people who have come to the end of themselves and who trust solely in the strength and the goodness of God. People who no longer have to appear "all together" but who can admit their weakness and make themselves vulnerable. People who have learned that what matters most is not what they accomplish but how much they love. Anyone who wants to be fully and powerfully used by God must be humbled. And the most humbling place on earth is the wilderness. For that reason, God's plan sometimes leads us to the last place we want to go. But when it does, it's always for our good.

However we get there, all of us must go through the wilderness in this life. When it's our turn, we don't have to ask, "Why are you doing this to me, God? Don't you love me anymore?" The truth is that everyone in this world has hard times; everyone is tested by life and its problems. Whether you enter the wilderness by your own mistakes, the actions of others, the flow of life, or God's purposeful plan, you can rest assured that God will teach and transform you through your wilderness experience. God is watching. He knows how you are struggling, and he has promised that he will not leave you or forsake you. As the old hymn so beautifully expresses, when you walk through the wilderness, God will "be with thee, thy trouble to bless, and sanctify to thee thy deepest distress."[2]

God has not promised to keep us out of the wilderness. But he has promised to be there with us and to use our wilderness to make us stronger in our faith and more like his Son.

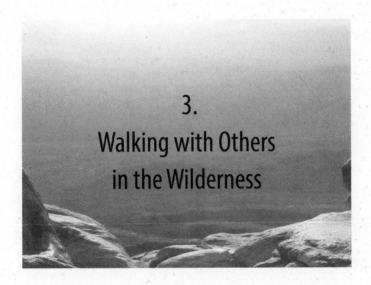

3.
Walking with Others
in the Wilderness

3.
Walking with Others in the Wilderness

As Americans, we value the archetypal image of "the rugged individualist." He or she is the person who is self-reliant and strong, facing life's challenges alone and unafraid. As Christians, we know there's more to life than that. We know that we are to rely on God, ask for his help, and through faith do "all things through him who strengthens me" (Philippians 4:13 NRSV). When we put the two ideas together, the tendency is to believe that "God and me" is all I need. I've got God. I've got the Bible. I've got my faith. What more do I need to live a faithful Christian life?

What we sometimes fail to appreciate is how important our relationships with other people are for growing spiritually and following Jesus. The idea of living for God without living in community may appeal to our sense of rugged individualism, but it is completely foreign to what the Scriptures teach. The Bible tells us to love one another (John 15:12), serve one another (Galatians 5:13), bear one another's burdens (Galatians 6:2), instruct one another (Romans 15:14), and encourage one another (1 Thessalonians 4:18; Hebrews 10:25). Why? Because life is about relationships—our relationship with God and our relationships with others.

When Jesus was asked what matters most in life, his answer was about relationships. He said that what is essential is loving God with the entirety of our being and loving others as ourselves (Matthew 22:36-40). Before we talk about the most important relationship—

our relationship with God—I want to explore in this chapter our relationships with others. To be faithful to God's calling in our lives, we will need the love and the instruction and the encouragement that come from others. We also will need to serve other people and bear their burdens.

The Christian life was never meant to be "God and me." It's "God and me and others." God is the one who transforms our hearts, but very often he uses other people to do his work in our lives. So relationships are always important. But in the wilderness, relationships are not only important; they are critical. In the most difficult times of life— when your heart is heavy, your spirit is depleted, and your future looks bleak and barren—your relationships with other people can make or break you. If anyone can teach us about this, it's Moses.

For forty years Moses walked in the wilderness with the Israelites, including a few who encouraged and assisted him and many who constantly misjudged his motives and attacked his integrity. Moses was not a perfect man, but how he walked with the Israelites, trusted in God, and continued to love those who often were ungrateful and angry has much to teach us about walking with others in our own wilderness. Let's consider some of the lessons we can learn from Moses.

Look to the People Who Can Help You

One thing we learn from Moses is the importance of looking to others. Moses was a man of great strength and knowledge. Being raised as a prince in Pharaoh's court, he would have received a world-class education. But he also is described as being "more humble than anyone else on the face of the earth" (Numbers 12:3). In the wilderness, his humility served him every bit as much as his strength and knowledge.

On several different occasions Moses asked for the help of others. The first was when he was setting out into the wilderness with the Israelites after bringing them out of Egypt. God led them in a visible way as they made their exodus, going before them as a pillar of cloud during the day and as a pillar of fire at night. The presence of God led them to Mount Sinai where he gave them the Law. God had fulfilled every promise he had made to Moses. He had acted powerfully to deliver the Israelites. He had led them visibly as they made their escape to Mount Sinai.

While they were camped there, waiting for God's direction, they were joined by Moses' in-laws. When God told Moses that it was time to leave Mount Sinai and push through the wilderness, Moses did something that might appear strange, even lacking in faith. He asked his brother-in-law Hobab,[1] a Midianite, to lead them in the wilderness. The Midianites were desert nomads. The wilderness was their natural habitat. They knew everything there was to know about the wilderness, including how to get through it safely and quickly.

When Moses asked Hobab to go with them, Hobab responded, "'No, I will not go; I am going back to my own land and my own people.' But Moses said, 'Please do not leave us. You know where we should camp in the wilderness, and you can be our eyes'" (Numbers 10:30-31).

God had told Moses that he would lead the Israelites and go before them. Even as Moses was talking to Hobab, the pillar of cloud was within sight. The very presence of God was there, ready to lead them into the wilderness. Some commentators have said that Moses made a mistake by asking Hobab to lead them. They suggest that asking for someone else to lead the Israelites was a lack of faith on Moses' part—that instead of trusting God, he put his faith in a man. But I don't see it that way.

I believe that when you are in the wilderness, God is going to be gracious and bring people into your life who can help you—people who know what you don't know; people who have been there before you. Just as God brought Hobab to Moses, God will bring into your life someone who knows the terrain and challenges you are facing. God will place someone in the middle of your wilderness who has been there before you, knows the way through, and will teach you the lessons that you need to learn. It's never a lack of faith to look to the people God puts into your life so that you can make your journey through the wilderness well.

Moses knew what he knew. He knew that he had the skills of a leader. He knew that he had a relationship with God. He knew that God had a plan for Israel. But just as important, Moses knew what he didn't know, and he had the humility to ask his brother-in-law to help him. Imagine how hard that must have been for Moses: "Hobab, you know where there's water in the wilderness. I don't. You know where there's vegetation for our animals. I don't. You know which routes are safe. I don't. Come and be our eyes in the wilderness." If Moses was weak because he needed help, I believe he also was strong because he was willing to ask for the help he needed.

Knowing what you don't know is wisdom. Being willing to admit what you don't know is humility. Overcoming your pride and asking for the help you need is great strength. In fact, it's one of the characteristics of every great leader.

This reminds me of a quote from one of my favorite contemporary theologians. You may not be familiar with the names of many contemporary theologians, but you'll probably know this one: Clint Eastwood. In his movie *Magnum Force*, Eastwood's character, Harry Callahan, says, "A man's got to know his limitations." If you want to be a child, you don't have to know your limitations. If you're content being an adolescent, you can tell yourself that you know just about everything and can handle just about anything that comes your way. But if you want to be a grown-up man or woman, you have to know your limitations and be willing to ask for help. As the band U2 sang, "Sometimes you can't make it on your own."[2] One of those times is when you're in the wilderness.

Maybe you entered a place of devastation when the doctor said, "It's cancer." Maybe your time in the wilderness began when someone close to you rejected or betrayed you. Maybe it was when you lost a job. Some of us entered the wilderness when a child we loved began to make self-destructive choices and nothing we tried to do seemed to help. However your wilderness began, there is someone who has been there before you and who has learned the lessons you need to learn. Saying to yourself, "I don't need that kind of help—and even if I do, I won't ask for it," doesn't make you strong. Actually, it makes you weak and foolish—especially if others are counting on you just as the Israelites were depending on Moses. And whether or not you know it, someone *is* depending on you to make it through your wilderness the right way.

If you are to get the help you need in the wilderness, you probably will have to overcome a few things. I'd like to suggest four common obstacles.

1. Self-pity

A common mistake we make in the wilderness is focusing on our problems instead of looking at our resources. Perhaps we think there is no one who is willing to help us. Remember Elijah? That's how he felt when he prayed to die in the wilderness after telling God, "I alone am left" (1 Kings 19:10 NRSV). Elijah felt that his enemy was great, his strength was little, and he was all alone. That's often how we feel in the wilderness, too. But recall what God told Elijah— that there were seven thousand others who had not bent the knee to Baal and who would stand with him and help him in the battles ahead.

One day my receptionist came into my office and said, "Rob, there's a woman in the reception area who is crying and who needs to see a pastor." That's how I met Stephanie. She had stopped crying as she stepped into my office, but she began sobbing again as soon as she sat down. Finally she was able to tell me what had happened. Her husband had cheated on her. He had told her that he didn't love her and never had. Then he had moved out and left her with the kids to raise.

Stephanie told me about her children and how much she loved them, how hard it had been at work, and how she had been praying for God to help her. She also told me that she had been crying for two months. "I can't stop," she said. "I'm all alone, I don't have anyone to help me, and I have lost everything." After listening for an hour, I told her that I couldn't imagine the pain she was in and that I cared.

When she told me again that she couldn't stop crying, I gently said to her, "Stephanie, you won't stop crying until you start believing what's true about yourself."

"What do you mean?" she asked.

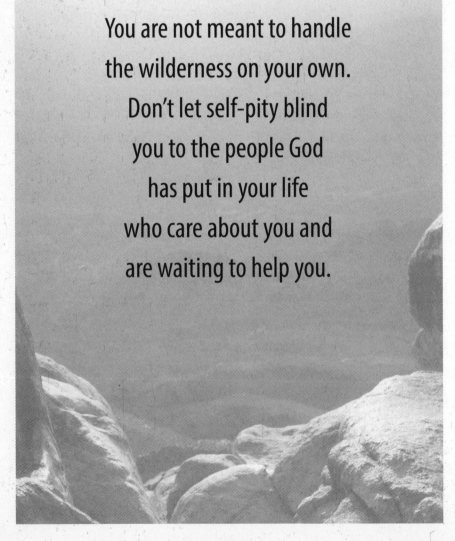

You are not meant to handle
the wilderness on your own.
Don't let self-pity blind
you to the people God
has put in your life
who care about you and
are waiting to help you.

I said, "You just told me that you've lost everything. You told me that because that's what you believe. But that's not true."

Again she asked, "What do you mean?"

"Have you lost your health?" I asked her.

"No," she said tentatively.

"Have you lost the children who mean more to you than life?"

"No."

"Have you lost your job? Or your ability to learn or to love or to live above your circumstances?"

"No."

"Have you lost your relationship with God?"

"No, I haven't," she said.

I looked at her and said, "Stephanie, you have lost more than I ever have. I can't imagine how painful this must be. And it's good that you have cried about it. But when you want to stop crying and move forward, you will have to stop believing what's false and start believing what's true. God loves you and will never leave you. You still have what's most important to you. And God and you can get through anything."

She quit crying, and we made a plan for her to meet with a counselor and become connected to our divorce care ministry. We met other times, and I helped her find a Sunday morning group where she received the nurture and care she needed. Her relationship with God blossomed, joy returned to her life, and I had the privilege of conducting the wedding ceremony for her and a wonderful man who had seen the beautiful person she was and had fallen in love with her.

As human beings, we suffer great hurts. And when we do, it's easy to think that we have lost everything and have no one to help us. If that's you, I want to say this as tenderly to you as I did to Stephanie: that's not true. You still have much to live for, you have more strength than you know, and there are people who will be glad to stand with you and help you fight your battles if only you will ask. What can keep you from finding those people is the self-pity that says, "No one cares; I'm all alone." You are not meant to handle the wilderness on your own. Don't let self-pity blind you to the people God has put in your life who care about you and are waiting to help you.

2. *Pride*

Another obstacle is pride, which says, "I can handle this on my own." If you could handle the wilderness on your own, you'd get out quickly, right? You wouldn't linger there, hurting and struggling and wondering how long you will feel the way you do.

Thirteen years ago I began a ministry for men in our community. Now, each week five hundred men listen to me talk about what it means to seek God as men, fathers, and husbands. I can't count the number of times that men have spoken to me about their lives. I have learned much. Most men want to be good husbands and fathers, for example. But one thing I know for sure from listening to the hearts of men is this: most men are lonely. Most men don't have a close friend, and the reason they don't is because they will not open up about their hurts, fears, and failures. Being respected is incredibly important to men. And they are afraid that if they show their weaknesses, they will lose the respect of other men. So, they put up walls around their hearts like a fortress, thinking they will be safe, only to find that they have created a prison where they are alone.

I know many women struggle with loneliness, as well. When so many of us live far from our extended families, commute long distances each day to work, and frequently move to new communities pursuing a career, it's understandable that people are lonely and feel disconnected from others. But I'm thinking about a different phenomenon. There are people who have lived in the same community, held the same job, and gone to the same church for years. Still they feel isolated and alone.

Why? Because they are afraid to be vulnerable with another human being. They are afraid that they will be rejected if they allow another person to see them as they are. And at the core of it is pride. Pride makes us afraid of reaching out, opening up, and being found out. As a result, it makes us lonely. It closes us off to the people who could help us if only we would ask, and it causes us to stay longer in the wilderness than we have to. For some of us, pride keeps us in the wilderness all our lives.

Getting over the pride that says we don't need any help is critical. All pride ever does is trap us into making the same mistakes again and again. Life isn't intended to be lived alone. Let go of your pride if you want to step out of the wilderness and take hold of life.

3. False Humility

Another obstacle we may need to overcome is false humility. The strangest thing happens when people make an appointment to see me about a hurt they've suffered or a problem they're facing. After they finish telling me about it and I look them in the eyes and say that what they're facing sounds terribly difficult and painful and my heart goes out to them, almost invariably they respond, "That's okay. It's not that bad." They made an appointment to see me, sat down in my office, took a deep breath, started with the words, "I don't know where to begin...," and used half a box of tissues as they told me about their situation. But "it's not that bad." If your problems are bad enough for you to open up and tell someone about them, they're bad.

You might say, "Well, my problems are not as bad as other people's." Perhaps, but what difference does that make? That's like someone who has been stabbed in the leg—who is bleeding and walking around with a hand pressed on the wound—saying, "I don't think I'll go to the emergency room because there are people who have been shot in the chest, and they have it a lot worse than I do. Compared to them, I don't have anything to complain about." Does it make any sense for that person to say, "There are people who are suffering worse than I am, so I'm not going to bother anyone and ask for help? I'll just walk around wounded, limping for the rest of my life?" Of course not! But we often do that very thing with our spiritual and emotional wounds, don't we? We often do that when life is overwhelming and our hearts are broken. We often do that when the wilderness seems to go on forever and we begin to lose hope. *Others have it worse*, we think to ourselves, *so I shouldn't bother anyone with my needs. My problems aren't that bad, and my wilderness isn't that big.*

61

That kind of thinking is false humility. The crazy, unfathomable love of God says that each of us is worth the life of his Son, Jesus. You don't get to decide if you are worthy of someone else's attention or help or kindness. You are! God says you are. And, even if he allows you to be in the wilderness for a time, he wants you to get the help you need while you're there so that you can learn and grow and step out of the wilderness whole and strong. False humility does not honor God. It dishonors him. To get the help we need in the wilderness, we must overcome false humility.

4. False Spirituality

A fourth obstacle we may have to overcome is false spirituality, which we talked about at the beginning of the chapter. This is the mistaken spirituality that says, "Because I have a relationship with God, I don't really need others in my life. I should be able to handle this on my own." There are a few rare occasions when it may be just you and God. But that's not how he intended us to live life. What did he say about Adam before sin entered the world, when he lived not in a wilderness but in a paradise? "It is not good for the man to be alone" (Genesis 2:18). Adam had God, but God knew Adam needed another person to share his life with.

The Apostle Paul was closer to God and stronger emotionally than most of us ever will be, but when he was in prison and saw his martyrdom approaching, he wrote these words to his son in the faith, Timothy: "Do your best to come to me quickly" (2 Timothy 4:9). Paul was in the wilderness of his approaching death. In that same letter to Timothy, Paul wrote about those who had deserted him and essentially said to Timothy, "I need to see your face. I need to hear your voice. I need you with me so that I can die a death that honors my God. Come as quickly as you can."

Even Jesus took three disciples to be with him as he wrestled in prayer in the garden of Gethsemane (Matthew 26:37). Our Lord felt the need of human companionship and the support of friends when he faced the most difficult challenge of his life. His example tells us that when we come to our wilderness, we should not try to face it alone.

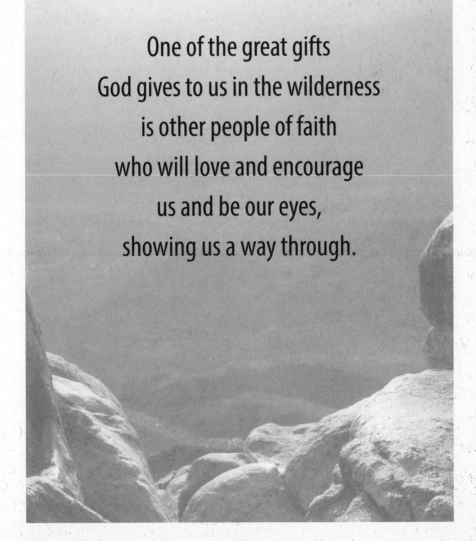

One of the great gifts
God gives to us in the wilderness
is other people of faith
who will love and encourage
us and be our eyes,
showing us a way through.

Like it or not, God made us with a need for other people. Becoming a Christian and living a life of faith doesn't change that. And one of the great gifts God gives to us in the wilderness is other people of faith who will love and encourage us and be our eyes, showing us a way through. True spirituality looks for that gift and accepts it when it comes.

Jennifer was a lovely young woman who was happily married and had two beautiful children. In a single moment, her life was changed forever. The phone rang, and she was told that her husband had been killed in a car accident coming home from work. In a split second she stepped out of a life of promise, abundance, and joy into a world of pain, confusion, and fear. In the days that followed, she wondered, *How am I going to make it? I'm without the love of my life, and my sons are without their father. How will we ever make it through this wilderness?*

I met with Jennifer and her sons immediately after they learned of Tom's death. I tried to console them and prayed with them. In the next few weeks, I met with her several times in my office. Eventually, she began to attend a grief workshop at a nearby hospital. A couple of months passed, and I asked her how she was. She told me, "I'm doing better now. I think I'm going to make it." When I inquired if the grief group was helping and she said yes, I asked her to tell me about the person who led the group. Jennifer said, "She's a really fine woman. She has her masters in social work. She's very capable, really insightful, and good at leading the group." I thought she was done, but after a moment, she continued. "But she's not the one who has helped me most. There are two older women in the group, both widows. They're there to support people like me. Both of them lost their husbands when they were my age. And they had children close to my boys' ages when their husbands died. It's what they have said about their experiences that has been the most helpful. Learning from their stories has given me the confidence that I can get through this."

Who better to help a grieving wife and mother than those who had been in that same wilderness and made it through? There is no better help than those who can say to her, "I remember the fear that was in my heart. I remember how worried I was for my children.

I know what it's like not having the strength to get out of bed and face the day, much less the rest of my life. But God got me through. I will never be over my loss, but life is good again. And what God did for me, he will do for you."

Who better to help someone who has lost a job than someone who's been there? I often say in sermons, "Trust God. Don't depend on the provision; rely on the Provider. If you lose your job, trust that God has something better for you." All of this is true. But it's even better if there is someone who can say, "I remember when I was let go. I know what it's like to feel lost and to have no idea what to do next. I remember the issues of self-esteem I struggled with. But God got me through, and life is better than it was before." The person who has lost a job and has made it through has the spiritual authority to speak into someone else's life. The person who has been there can give more hope than any sermon I could ever preach.

Who better to help the alcoholic than another alcoholic? Only someone who knows the struggle of alcoholism can look someone in the eyes and say, "I remember being right where you are. I remember how alcohol was my best friend and my greatest shame. It promised life but brought devastation. I remember that terrible, awful moment when it hit me that I could never drink again. And it put such fear in my heart because I couldn't imagine another day without a drink— much less the rest of my life. But God has brought me out of the wilderness into a Promised Land that is better than anything I ever imagined. I can look myself in the mirror and not be ashamed. I can look people in the eye and not be embarrassed. What God did for me, he'll do for you. If you'll let me, I'll walk through this wilderness with you, being your eyes and teaching you what I have learned."

Whatever wilderness you are in, don't make the mistake of trying to walk through it alone. There are other people who are willing to help you. They want to help you. People who have been in the wilderness and have come out of it have a heart for those who are in the same kind of wilderness. They understand. They don't judge. They tell you the truth you need to hear. They encourage you to do the right things. They walk with you, being your eyes and showing you the way.

One reason Moses succeeded so beautifully in the wilderness was his willingness to ask for help. Learn from his example. Look to the people God brings who can help you, and ask for the help you need.

Forgive the People Who Hurt You

Another lesson we can learn from Moses is to forgive the people who have hurt us.

During the forty years he walked with the Israelites in the wilderness, listening to the complaints of the people, Moses must have asked God a thousand times, "What did I do to deserve this?" The grumbling started immediately as they left Egypt. No sooner than you could say, "Free at last, free at last, I thank God I'm free at last,"[3] the Israelites began to complain: "Moses, why did you drag us out into this wilderness? It was better in Egypt. Moses, if you were going to set us free, you should have planned better. We don't have enough water. We don't like the food. Moses, why did you make us leave Egypt where we had it so good?"

Moses had left everything he had known, stepped out in faith, challenged Pharaoh, and risked his life for them. And instead of gratitude, he received criticism and condemnation. Moses had every right to look at them and say, "Listen, I'm the one who dreamed for you when nobody else would. I'm the one who believed you could be free when no one else did. When you were in Egypt wondering why God had forgotten you, I'm the one he sent. I'm the one who pointed a finger in the face of Pharaoh and demanded, 'Let my people go.' And all you do is complain and grumble against me. If you think you're better off without me, go your own way and see how that works out for you."

Moses had every right to say those things, but he didn't. We talk about the patience of Job, but it's the patience of Moses that amazes me. He continued to love and serve and lead his people no matter how they grumbled or criticized or even conspired against him.

It's difficult when someone you don't know is unfair to you, misjudges you, or misrepresents you to others. But when people you have loved and served turn on you, say things that are untrue and hurtful, and forget every good thing you've done for them, that's when the wounds are the deepest. Maybe a child looks at you and says, "You've never done anything for me. Everything you think you've done for me was for you." Or perhaps a spouse explains his or her affair as if it is your fault, saying that you weren't who you were supposed to be. When the wounds of rejection and accusation come from someone you have cared for and sacrificed for, they cut deep and linger long. This is hard to say, because the wilderness is difficult enough already, but if you want to move forward with God in the wilderness, you need to learn to forgive.

Moses was amazing in this regard. Over and over he continued to love and care for the people who were critical of him. On five different occasions as the Israelites were wandering through the wilderness, God grew weary of the Israelites and their constant complaining. He told Moses in so many words, "I'm changing the script. I'm going to bring my wrath upon these ungrateful malcontents and bring an end to them. From here on out, Moses, it's going to be you and me. We'll find a people who appreciate what we do for them, and we'll start over."

The first time God told Moses that he was done with the people of Israel was when Moses was encountering God on Mount Sinai. God told Moses that the Israelites had made a golden calf and were worshiping it. Then God said, "They are a stiff-necked people. Now leave me alone so that my anger may burn against them and that I may destroy them. Then I will make you into a great nation" (Exodus 32:9-10).

If I were Moses, I would have been tempted to say something like this: "God, would you repeat that last part about a great nation? Get rid of them and make me into a great nation? That's your plan? God, I like it. I like it a lot. What took you so long to come up with this? Let's start over and see what the two of us can do without these losers."

Now, I really wouldn't have said that. I might have thought it, but I wouldn't have said it. But I might have said, "God, we don't need to go nuclear here. How about this? Boils all over their bodies for two weeks—the kind that really hurt. And if they ever get out of line again, I'll say, 'Remember the boils?' And they'll straighten up right away."

But Moses did not respond the way I might have. "Moses sought the favor of the LORD his God. 'LORD,' he said, 'why should your anger burn against your people, whom you brought out of Egypt.... Turn from your fierce anger; relent and do not bring disaster on your people' " (Exodus 32:11-12). Absolutely amazing. Moses forgave the people, pleaded for God to be merciful to them, and continued to love and serve them. And he did this not once but several times. I believe this is one reason Moses was successful as he made his way through the wilderness.

When you are in the midst of life's most devastating experiences, you do not have a spare ounce of physical, emotional, mental, or spiritual energy to waste. In the wilderness you must be constantly looking for where God is leading you and what he is trying to teach you. If you are focused on what was done to you in the past, you will not be able to see what God is doing in the present. If you give your strength to the hurts you suffered yesterday, you will not have the strength you need to overcome the challenges you're facing today. Forgiveness is difficult when your wounds are deep. But it is essential if you want to move forward and come out of the wilderness healthy and whole.

Simply stated, forgiveness is letting someone who owes you something go free. It's being able within your spirit to look at someone and say, "You don't owe me anything anymore. You don't owe me an apology. You don't owe me an explanation. You don't owe me amends. I let you go. I wish you well." Forgiving disloyalty and betrayal is never easy. But when you let the person who hurt you go free, you discover that you're the one who has been set free.

We do not fix the pain in our hearts by fixing the person who put it there. We fix the pain in our hearts by forgiving the person who put it there. That's the way out. Forgiving and forgetting are not the same things. Forgiving someone is not saying that what was done to us doesn't matter. It's not deciding that the other person does not deserve justice. Rather, it is a spiritual decision that cancels the emotional debt someone owes us. The result is that our hearts are healed, our souls are cleansed, and our spirits are lifted. We discover a new freedom to be present for what God wants to do in us and through us. If we make it through the wilderness without letting go of bitterness and anger and forgiving those who have hurt us, then even once we're out of the wilderness we still will have a wilderness within us, creating devastation where God means for there to be life.

I implore you to let go of your hurts. Forgive the people who have wounded you. You might say, "Well, Rob, you don't know what he or she did to me." You're right. I don't. But I know what choosing not to forgive is doing to you. Forgiveness is always important, and in the wilderness it's critical.

Sometimes people tell me that they don't want to forgive because they don't want to get back into the same relationship that caused them so much pain. God says that we must forgive, but God doesn't say that we have to be foolish. It's foolish to trust someone who has hurt you if he or she hasn't changed and is still untrustworthy. It is possible to forgive without reestablishing a relationship. But forgiving that person is important so that you can be set free from anger and bitterness and come out of the wilderness whole.

Let God Correct Those Who Judge You

A final lesson we learn from Moses is to leave the correction of our criticizers to God.

First let me say that we all need constructive criticism. Some of my best friends are those who have been willing to point out my flaws and correct me. We need to listen when someone says, "Here's something I think you need to look at in your life." When someone knows us and loves us, we need to pay attention to his or her correction.

Even if someone doesn't know us well, we need to listen to what the person has to say if he or she comes to us in the right spirit. "Rob, I saw you doing something, and it just doesn't line up with who I think you are. What were you thinking?" We should honor that kind of criticism because that kind of criticism honors us.

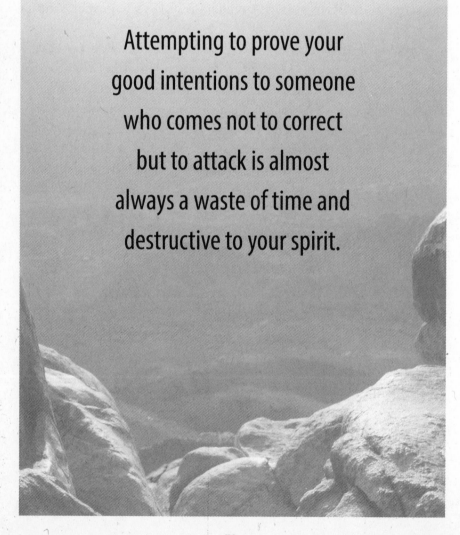

Attempting to prove your
good intentions to someone
who comes not to correct
but to attack is almost
always a waste of time and
destructive to your spirit.

But what we find in the wilderness is that when we're down and hurting, there will be people who come to us not with constructive criticism but with calculated condemnation. People will come not to build us up but to tear us down. There will be people who will tell us that we're in the wilderness because of something we have done or haven't done. They will tell us that we are merely getting what we deserve.

Most parents who have a child involved with drugs will have someone blame them for the way that they parented that child. Many women and men whose spouses cheated on them are told that if only they had been more caring or more attentive to their spouse's needs, he or she wouldn't have looked for love in the arms of someone else. In the wilderness, people may come to you not to build you up, not to teach you what you need to know, not to encourage you to keep learning and growing, but to rip into you with harsh words that are brutal, demeaning, and condemning. When that happens, the temptation is always to try to prove them wrong, and that temptation is almost always a mistake. Attempting to prove your good intentions to someone who comes not to correct but to attack is almost always a waste of time and destructive to your spirit.

Again, Moses is an example for us. The most difficult challenge he faced to his leadership was when 250 elders, led by three malcontents, leveled a series of charges against him that attacked his integrity. They told him that he was a failed leader. They charged him with being arrogant and deceiving the people. And they accused him of using his position for dishonest gain.

Moses had every right to vindicate himself. He could have rightly responded, "Without me, you were slaves. With me, you are free. Without me, you wondered why God had forgotten you. With me, God is right here with you—you see his presence in the cloud and in the pillar of fire. Without me, you would be in bondage forever. With me, you're on your way to the Promised Land. I could take everything you own, and you'd still owe me. But I haven't taken a thing of yours."

Moses could have defended himself. But he didn't. In fact, he turned from them to God and asked God to vindicate him. Moses did not live for an audience of many; he lived for an audience of One. So he spoke to God immediately after the elders attacked him, saying, "I have not taken so much as a donkey from them, nor have I wronged any of them" (Numbers 16:15). And God responded by siding with Moses. (You can read the full story in Numbers 16.)

People are unfair because they're unfair. People are brutal because they're brutal. People are condemning because they're condemning. These statements may sound trite, but they're actually profound. And they should give you freedom not to spend your time trying to win the favor of people who have chosen to attack you.

People who want to be fair will ask you for your side of the story before they judge you. People who are unfair could care less and won't be swayed by what you have to say. People who are brutal are not brutal because they have the wrong idea of what's going on inside of you—of your desires and your motives. They are brutal because of what's going on inside of them—their anger and jealousy. People who condemn you are rarely driven by who you are but by who they are—insecure and judgmental.

Don't live for your critics. Live for your Creator. Don't seek to please those who attack you. Live to please the One you hope one day to hear say, "Well done, good and faithful servant." His is the opinion that matters.

There have been times when I have blocked people on my e-mail or social media—not many, just a few. After I considered their criticism and did my best to respond with respect and compassion but the barrage just kept coming, I decided that continuing the conversation was unproductive and unhealthy—certainly for me and probably for them. When I have shared this suggestion with others, some have said, "I could never do that." Actually, it's not that hard. You write, "I have considered your comments. It looks like we're going to disagree on this. God bless you." Then you hit "send." Then you hit "block." It's that easy.

I've told people I've counseled to block certain people from their phones and never to take another call from those individuals. There are those who might say, "Rob, that doesn't seem very nice. It doesn't sound very Christian." But if they were to hear what I've heard—words meant to rip the heart out of someone, attacks meant to destroy a person's worth—they might change their minds.

Sometimes it is right and very Christian for us to say, "I have boundaries in my life. Period." Sometimes it's right to say, "I may not be perfect, but I am a child of God; and no child of God should be abused or demeaned." Jesus was crucified for you. So you don't need to allow other people to crucify you for no good reason. In fact, you have every right to say, "I am going to live for God's opinion; I'm not going to spend my time with those who would criticize and condemn me unfairly."

I cannot think of a single time that Jesus was concerned with what others thought about him. He knew that his coming into the world would divide people into two camps—those for him and those against him. He didn't change his message when he was called a blasphemer; he didn't defend his integrity when he was charged with breaking the law; he did not become defensive when his association with society's "undesirables" was called into question. He simply continued to teach the truth, do the Father's will, and open his arms to all who would receive him.

Jesus spent no time trying to convince those who attacked him that he was right and they were wrong. He opened his heart to those who came with questions, even those who doubted. But he had no codependent desires for everyone to like him or even understand him. Those who criticized him unfairly could look at his life. If they chose to attack his integrity, his compassion and his concern for the poor as blasphemy and the work of the evil one, then he would spend no time trying to convince them that they were wrong.

You don't have to convince your critics, either. You don't have to prove yourself to people who are unfair and condemning. Put your focus on God. Be faithful to what he has told you to do. Live for the approval of the One to whom you will one day answer. And he, with the help of others, will see you through.

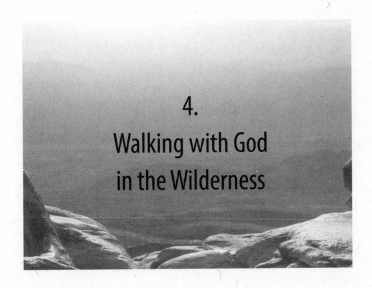

4.
Walking with God
in the Wilderness

4.
Walking with God in the Wilderness

We've seen that relationships are critical for us to make it through the wilderness God's way, coming out on the other side strong, healthy, and whole. And no relationship is more important in or out of the wilderness than our relationship with God. How do we maintain and grow our connection with God when life is full of pain and the future seems bleak? Once again, Moses has much to teach us.

One of the reasons I have come to love Moses is because he was a man of great passion—someone who, in spite of obstacles and opposition, was fully committed to a great purpose. At the core of this great purpose—leading God's people out of slavery and into the Promised Land—was his greatest passion: walking with his God. Deep within Moses' heart was the desire to experience and remain in the presence of God. Despite forty years in the wilderness with people who constantly grumbled against him and at times conspired to put him to death, he still found the strength to love them and lead them. His ability to be faithful to his calling came from his intimate relationship with God. Let's explore what we can learn from Moses about walking with God in the wilderness.

Walk in Faith

First, walking with God in the wilderness means walking in faith.

In the wilderness, our lives often don't make sense. Though we've talked generally about why God allows us to walk through the wilderness, we usually do not understand what's happening to us when we're in the midst of it, much less why. The "not knowing" is often what is most difficult about the wilderness. How long will it continue? What's the point of all this suffering? Why would God allow us to go through this? If we are to remain connected and close to God, we must come to the place spiritually where we can say, "I may not know what's happening, but I believe God does. I believe God is with me. I believe God is working in me and for me. And I believe God will get me through."

In the wilderness, we will walk either by faith or by feelings. If we base our lives on how we feel—singled out, hopeless, confused, angry—we not only will fail to learn the lessons of the wilderness but also will eventually lose the strength and focus we need to move forward. But if, in spite of our feelings and circumstances, we live by faith in God and his promises—promises such as "I know the plans I have for you ... plans for good and not for disaster" (Jeremiah 29:11 NLT), "In all things God works for the good of those who love him" (Romans 8:28), and "Surely I am with you always, to the very end of the age" (Matthew 28:20)—then we will find God faithful and his grace sufficient. Walking in faith means we don't have to understand what's happening to us or why. We simply need to hold on to the truth that God is faithful even when life doesn't make sense. As the popular saying often attributed to Charles Spurgeon affirms, when we cannot trace God's hand, we can trust his heart.

After the Israelites had endured four hundred years of bondage in Egypt, God sent Moses to deliver them. When Pharaoh refused to let them go, God acted powerfully to bring judgment upon the Egyptians until the children of Israel were given their freedom. They made their exodus to Mount Sinai where they received the Law. Then they pushed through the wilderness quickly and came to the Promised Land. Moses knew there were enemies in the land, so he sent twelve spies on a reconnaissance mission. They were to come back with a report concerning the tribes who lived there.

Ten of the twelve spies reported that the land was, as promised, incredibly abundant and desirable. But they also agreed that the Israelites could never defeat the people who lived there. Their report went something like this: "They're bigger and stronger than we are. They outnumber us and are better equipped. We could never take them. We should turn around and go back to Egypt."

The people in the camp were demoralized by the report. The general consensus was that living in slavery was preferable to dying in the Promised Land. Like the soldier in the movie *Braveheart* who rejected William Wallace's call for the men of Scotland to fight for their freedom, the Israelites responded, "Fight? Against that? No! We will run. And we will live."

Then the two other spies, Joshua and Caleb, spoke up. "We agree," they said. "It is true that the people we will face are numerous and strong. But you should see the land. It's rich and fertile. It's flowing with milk and honey. Most important, God has promised it to us. If we only go forward, he will fight our battles and make a way for us."

At this point, the Israelites suddenly became the world's first democracy. They took a vote, and in a landslide victory, they decided to return to Egypt. For good measure, they determined to stone Caleb, Joshua, and Moses to death and be done with those who were calling them to step into a future of promise.

Finally, God had had enough and said, "How long will these people treat me with contempt? How long will they refuse to believe in me?" (Numbers 14:11).

If we could ask the Israelites why they refused to step into the future God had prepared for them, they probably would have said, "It's because of all the people in the land—how big they are, how strong they are, how well-equipped they are." And if we pressed them a bit, they might have been more honest and told us that what was keeping them out of the Promised Land was the fear within them. But God went even deeper when he asked, "How long will they refuse to believe in me?" In other words, "What's keeping you from the Promised Land is not how great your enemies are but how small your faith in me is."

God turned them around and sent them back into the wilderness where they wandered, struggled, and suffered for forty years. Why? To teach them faith. To take everything away from them and humble them so that they would learn to trust in him and act in faith. Very often that is exactly what the wilderness does to us.

Outside of the wilderness our faith may grow in any number of ways. We read the Bible, spend time with others who have faith, pray, and see God answer our prayers; and our faith steadily grows. But inside the wilderness, God uses another means to grow our faith. He humbles us and brings us to our knees. In the wilderness, it may seem that everything has been taken from you—your success, your confidence, your ability to make sense of your world, and sometimes even your health, finances, or friends. When you have nothing and no one to depend on but God, that's when you discover that God is enough. When you are stripped of everything but the promises of God and your faith, that's when you learn that "the grass withers and the flowers fall, / but the word of our God endures forever" (Isaiah 40:8). It's when we are on our faces, humbled by our inability to make our lives work, much less save ourselves, that we seek God unlike any other time in our lives. And that is when God can impress deeply into our hearts the truth that his Word can always be trusted. That's what the wilderness is meant to teach us, so that in both good times and bad times we will place our faith in God alone.

Why was Moses able to walk with God in faith throughout the Israelites' wilderness wanderings? Because, as we learned in the previous chapter, Moses was a very humble man. He had been humbled in a previous wilderness experience. Remember the story with me. Moses was born an Israelite but raised as a prince in Pharaoh's court, and he grew to be a man of great position, power, and influence. When he discovered that in reality he was an Israelite, he began to identify with his people and their suffering. One day he saw an Egyptian mistreating two Israelites, and he acted rashly, striking and killing the Egyptian. Fearing that Pharaoh would learn he was actually an Israelite, Moses escaped into the wilderness.

The man who once had everything now had nothing. The man who once had position and prominence now lived in obscurity.

For forty years Moses lived humbly in the wilderness with God. There he married and raised sheep and learned the lessons of the wilderness—that if God is all you have, you have enough; that it's better to have nothing with God than to have position and prominence without God; that when you come to the end of yourself, you can have a new beginning with God. These are lessons we all need to learn.

If you have trusted your wealth—if money gives you a sense of security and identity—then God is likely to allow you to experience a wilderness where all the wealth in the world will do you no good. If you have trusted your intellect—if your wits and knowledge make you feel safe and confident you can handle anything that comes your way—expect a wilderness where your wisdom will be utterly insufficient for what you're facing. If you have trusted your looks, charm, or past successes, be prepared for a time when none of those will be sufficient to overcome the problems you are facing. Before you can be fully used or blessed by God, you must come to that place where you have nothing but him. There God will say to you, "Trust me—not what you feel, not what you see, not what makes sense, not what has worked before. Trust me."

Sometimes the wilderness will strip from you even the sense that God is with you. Even then God will say to you, "Trust me. When you pray and you don't feel my presence, trust me, not your feelings. When you cry out and it seems I'm not listening, trust me. When I ask you to fight a battle that appears too big for you or tell you to take a step that puts fear in your heart, trust me."

The wilderness is meant to bring each of us to the place where we say, "I don't understand my life. I don't know why I'm here or why God would ask me to walk through this, but I choose to trust him." It's in the frightening, overwhelming, confusing moments of life where we discover that God is always enough.

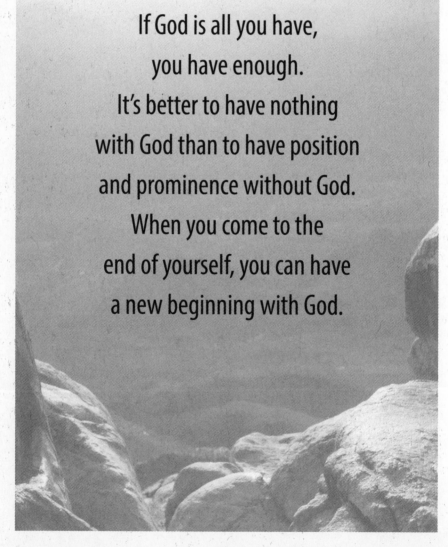

If God is all you have,
you have enough.
It's better to have nothing
with God than to have position
and prominence without God.
When you come to the
end of yourself, you can have
a new beginning with God.

In an earlier chapter I told you about my friend Brad, who died of cancer. Brad went through a wilderness where his disease and his life didn't make sense to him, and I watched him wrestle with himself, with his faith, and with God. As I knew it would, his faith grew stronger and the beautiful spirit within him returned. In the last few months of his life, he was able to comfort and encourage, in very powerful ways, others who were struggling.

Five months before Brad's death, an older man who had been diagnosed with cancer and was absolutely devastated by the news came to see me. After listening to the man, I told him about Brad and asked if he would like for Brad to contact him. He said that he would. Here is an excerpt from the encouraging letter that Brad wrote:

> Although I don't know you, I think I may know how you feel. Hearing the news that you have cancer raises a lot of questions. I think I asked them all. I was shocked, disappointed, angry, sad, confused, and depressed. At the time, that worried me. I wondered if maybe I didn't really have faith, or at least if I didn't have the faith I needed to stand up to this challenge. I wondered if God would be mad at me if I asked a million questions. I wondered if God would be angry with me if I was angry with him—because I was. To make matters worse, I felt terrible physically. I didn't have the energy to go on some grand quest for faith. I felt stuck. I couldn't move forward emotionally or spiritually.
>
> I decided to pray. I found that to be very difficult. Before I had cancer it seemed easy. I prayed every day, sometimes several times a day, sometimes for long periods of time. Suddenly I couldn't really seem to pray at all. It felt as if God had deserted me when I needed him most. I always thought of prayer as a conversation. I sensed that God was listening and responding. Then when I had cancer and needed that sensation, it wasn't there. I felt like I was talking out in the darkness, and

there wasn't even an echo. But I resolved to go on praying. I decided to pray the Lord's Prayer every night. That was all I could do, and I didn't feel anything when I did it. I felt like I was hanging on to God and my faith by a thread.

Then I remembered a sermon I had heard. The pastor had said that God was as tenacious as a bulldog in holding on to us. It seemed important to me to visualize that God was holding on to me. I didn't have to do all the holding. I prayed, "God, I don't know if I can hold on to you; I guess you'll have to hold on to me." It was my first little breakthrough. I relaxed a little for the first time. I didn't suddenly start praying like mad and having great insights. I just relaxed a little and trusted God to hold on to me when I couldn't hold on to Him.

Sometimes it seems that the wilderness has taken everything from us, including our energy, the answers we've held on to, and even the sense that God is with us. Still God says, "Trust me." When we don't feel his presence, we can trust him. When we pray and don't know if he's there, we can trust him. When we cry out and he doesn't seem to answer, we can trust him. Why? Because he has promised, "I will never leave you or forsake you" (Hebrews 13:5 NRSV) and "My grace is sufficient for you" (2 Corinthians 12:9). Because of this, we can affirm with the Apostle Paul, "I can do all things through Christ who strengthens me" (Philippians 4:13 NKJV). If only we will trust God, he will work in and through us and do more than we could ever imagine.

You might be thinking, *But Brad died; he lost his battle with cancer.* You're right; Brad died. But he did not lose his battle with cancer. When you know that your life is coming to an end but you hold on to your faith; when nothing makes sense but you continue to pray; when you no longer feel the presence of God but you refuse to become bitter or give in to despair; when your body is racked with disease but what people remember is how you loved and encouraged them and taught them that God is faithful—when that's how you live the last months of your life, you win the battle with cancer. It doesn't defeat you; you defeat it.

If you're in the wilderness right now, trust God—not your feelings or what makes sense, but God alone. You will discover that he is there with you and will never give up on you. He will hold on to you even if you can't hold on to him. Walk in faith, and he will have his way in your life; and ultimately that way will be good.

Before we move on, I want to share with you what may be the greatest statement of faith in the Bible. Habakkuk was a prophet who cried out to God with the age-old question: Why do the wicked prosper but your people suffer? In other words, "Why is the world so unjust? God, why don't you act to make things right?" Then he said he would wait for God to give him an answer.

He did wait, but no answer came. At least none that explained why good people suffer or why God allows evil in the world. He was told only to trust God and his plan.

Without an explanation that satisfied his questions or answered his complaints, the prophet declared:

> Though the fig tree does not bud
>> and there are no grapes on the vines,
> though the olive crop fails
>> and the fields produce no food,
> though there are no sheep in the pen
>> and no cattle in the stalls,
> yet I will rejoice in the LORD,
>> I will be joyful in God my Savior.
>
>>>> (Habakkuk 3:17-18)

How did Habakkuk respond to the devastation and the suffering he saw around him? He said that he would trust in God—not in his abundance or lack thereof; not in his ability to make sense of his situation or to see a light at the end of the tunnel. When life was a wilderness and all he had were unanswered questions and a broken spirit, still he said he would trust in God and live by faith.

It's wonderful when our hearts are full of faith. We see our problems, but we have the assurance—like a great gift—that all will be well. This is when our feelings line up with our faith. But it's not always like that. Sometimes faith is a decision we make in spite of our feelings. Habakkuk's confession of faith was a decision to trust God when he had no answers. When the Israelites refused to enter the Promised Land, it was a decision *not* to act in faith. Moses, Caleb, and Joshua's willingness to move into the land in spite of the obstacles they clearly saw was a decision that God could be trusted. Faith is a decision to rise above our fears, our unanswered questions, and our sense of inadequacy and to trust God instead. If we listen to our feelings, we often will fail to move forward with God. But if we choose to act in faith, we will walk with God and eventually come to the place of blessing that he has for us.

Walk in Obedience

To walk with God in the wilderness also means to walk in obedience. Of course, it's when we're hurting that being obedient can be most difficult.

By definition, the wilderness is a time of pain and suffering. What I have learned from enduring my own wilderness experiences and from counseling hundreds of people in some kind of crisis is that when we are suffering, we will do almost anything to make the pain stop. It may be physical pain, but more often it's emotional or spiritual pain—such as the pain of feeling that we're all alone, that we've been deserted, that we've been misjudged, or that our best efforts are not appreciated. Or sometimes, as we've said, it's the pain of feeling abandoned by God.

What I've discovered is that when the pain is intense and ongoing, we tend to look for a way out. We try to find something that will change how we feel. We become open to temptations that otherwise we never would have considered. Some of us turn to drink or drugs. Others of us turn to pornography or an affair. Still others spend money we don't have on things we don't need. Feeling trapped and desperate, we look for a way to escape the pain we are experiencing and to change the way we feel. We may even turn to things that under different circumstances we easily would recognize as dangerous and choose to avoid.

In the wilderness, we can make some of our greatest mistakes. We can make choices that we will regret for the rest of our lives. And when we finally get out of the wilderness, which has brought us so much pain, we often discover that the choices we made there related to one area of our lives have devastated other parts of our lives— as well as the lives of others.

If you're in a wilderness, please take this to heart: you do not mature as a human being, much less as a Christian, by escaping your pain. In fact, maturity requires suffering. That's why James wrote, "Consider it pure joy, my brothers and sisters, whenever you face trials of many kinds, because you know that the testing of your faith produces perseverance. Let perseverance finish its work so that you may be mature and complete, not lacking anything" (James 1:2-4).

We grow not by finding an easy way out of our pain but by facing our suffering honestly. When life is hard and our spirits are hurting, we have a great opportunity to become more like Christ; but we can do this only if we are faithful to endure and to be obedient to what God is calling us to do. Even Jesus had to suffer in order to accomplish the Father's will and be our perfect example. In the Book of Hebrews we read, "In bringing many sons and daughters to glory, it was fitting that God, for whom and through whom everything exists, should make the pioneer of their salvation perfect through what he suffered" (2:10).

Moses did not live a perfect life as Jesus did, but he did live an exemplary life characterized by obedience. When his sister Miriam and his brother Aaron criticized him, God defended him with these words: "He is faithful in all my house" (Numbers 12:7). God told Miriam and Aaron that if anyone were to criticize Moses, it would be him, not them. But God told them that Moses had been faithful. He had been trustworthy and obedient.

We grow not by finding
an easy way out of our pain but
by facing our suffering honestly.
When life is hard and
our spirits are hurting,
we have a great opportunity
to become more like Christ.

Moses was not driven by a desire to be powerful or well known. His goal was not to be liked by others. His primary concern was not to escape the pain of leading people who constantly criticized, opposed, and even attacked him. He was not looking for an easy shortcut out of the wilderness that had become his life. He had one great passion, and that was to walk faithfully with God.

There's a beautiful passage in Exodus 33 that reveals Moses' heart. God had told Moses that he was pleased with him and wanted to bless him. Moses responded, "You have said, 'I know you by name and you have found favor with me.' If you are pleased with me, teach me your ways so I may know you and continue to find favor with you" (Exodus 33:12-13a).

Be honest. If you had been in Moses' shoes, what would you have asked of God? Financial security? Good health? Professional success? Keep my children safe and let them find happiness? Tell me the secret of being content and at peace?

Moses could have asked for any of these things, but he didn't. He asked only to know more about walking in the ways that would please his God. He said essentially, "If I have been obedient in the past, teach me how to be even more obedient in the future; that's all I ask."

If I had been Moses, I think I might have said, "God, if I have pleased you, make the Israelites appreciate the sacrifices I have made for them. Make them respect my leadership. Make the constant attacks stop." But not Moses. He did not ask that his life be made easy or that his sufferings cease. His one request was that he would make God proud. He said in effect, "God, if you want to be good to me, teach me how to walk before you so that when you look at me, there's a smile on your face and joy in your heart. I want to know that when you think of me, you think, 'Well done, good and faithful servant'" (Matthew 25:23). That was the one request Moses made of God because that was the greatest desire of his heart. And because pleasing God was his greatest desire, he was able to be obedient and faithful in the wilderness where often he was opposed, criticized, and attacked.

I have a question for you, and I believe it may be the most important question you'll ever answer. What do you want? I'm not asking what you need. We all have the same needs—air to breathe, water to drink, food to eat, someone to love, something to live for. When it comes to needs, we all are alike. It's your wants that make you different. Your wants determine what you give your life to and what you seek. So, the question is, what do you want? What is your greatest desire?

Great lives have a great passion. They seek after it when life is easy and when life is hard, when they are loved and when they are hated, when life is wonderful and when life is a wilderness. Jesus said his passion was glorifying the Father: "Now my soul is troubled, and what shall I say? 'Father, save me from this hour'? No, it was for this very reason I came to this hour. Father, glorify your name!" (John 12:27-28a). The Apostle Paul said that his greatest desire was "to know Christ and the power of his resurrection and the sharing of his sufferings" (Philippians 3:10 NRSV). For Moses, it was walking in the ways of God faithfully and obediently.

Your life will never be greater than the cause you live for. It will never rise above the passion that drives you. So I ask again, what do you want? If the desire of your heart is happiness, there will be times when you refuse to suffer the pain required to be obedient to God's will for your life. If the desire of your heart is financial security, you may refuse to make the sacrifices necessary to be faithful in serving God's kingdom. If it's being well thought of, you will struggle between two masters—One who will applaud you for doing what is right and the other who will praise you for doing what is expedient.

Unlike any other time in your life, the wilderness will expose the desires of your heart. What do you want? Happiness or holiness? Becoming comfortable or becoming Christlike? Being free to do whatever you desire or being faithful in doing all that God desires? An easy way out of the pain you're experiencing or a way through the pain that brings glory to God and makes you the person he created you to be?

When you are experiencing the pain of the wilderness, you may want to look for some way out. You may think, "Surely God will understand. Nobody should have to bear this. I can't take it anymore. If I just give in this one time, it'll be okay." When you find yourself in that position, I encourage you to be faithful just a little longer. Resist temptation one more day. Be obedient right then, right where you are, because one day you will say to yourself, "It was worth it." You will be able to look back and say, "In the most difficult time of my life, by God's grace, I was faithful. That's when something broken in me was made whole; something wrong in me was made right; something twisted in me was straightened out." Do not make a mistake that you'll regret and that will only create a greater wilderness for yourself and others. Instead, do all you can to be obedient when you're in the wilderness.

God has seen your struggles, and he cares. God knows all the ways you have turned away from temptation and have been obedient, and he is pleased with you. So while you are in the wilderness, why not pray as Moses did, "God, my one request is that I would be faithful to you. Teach me to walk in your ways, and give me the strength to be obedient."

Walk in God's Presence

Finally, in order to walk with God in the wilderness, we must walk in God's presence. I know that sounds redundant. What I mean by this is that when we are in the wilderness, we must be intentional about seeking God and opening our lives to his presence. Seeking God is always important, but it is critically important when we are in the wilderness. Why? Because God's presence can be particularly difficult for us to experience when life is dry and barren. The wilderness breeds discontent with ourselves and even with God. Often we find ourselves questioning God, becoming angry because of what he is allowing in our lives, and growing self-absorbed and bitter. Our hearts can become hard and cold when we most need them to be open and soft. So when we find ourselves in the wilderness, we must be especially intentional about seeking the presence of God.

Moses recognized the importance of being in God's presence. In fact, it was in the wilderness where he first experienced God's presence. Before he was used by God to lead the Israelites, he encountered the presence of the living God in the burning bush on Mount Sinai; and in that moment, God captured his heart. When we read Moses' story, we discover that wherever he went, he was constantly seeking to be in the real, manifest presence of God. He often stepped away from the crowds to be with God. He spent time alone with God on Mount Sinai and later in the tent of meeting. His mission was to lead the people of Israel, but his passion was to be in the presence of God.

On Mount Sinai, Moses met with God and received the Ten Commandments. Just as he was about to return to the Israelites and say, "Here's what God requires of you," God broke the news to him that the people had created an idol, a golden calf, and were worshiping it. Then God said, "Leave this place, you and the people you brought up out of Egypt, and go up to the land . . . flowing with milk and honey. But I will not go with you, because you are a stiff-necked people" (Exodus 33:1, 3).

Once again put yourself in Moses' place. Basically God had said, "Okay, Moses, same deal as before. You get the Promised Land. You get my protection, my power, and my provision. But you don't get me. You don't get my presence. Everything else stays the same, but I will not go with you."

How do you think you would you have responded? Moses said, "If your Presence does not go with us, do not send us up from here (Exodus 33:15). In other words, "God, if I have to choose between living in this devastation with you or in the land of promise without you, I take the wilderness. I will stay where you are, because more than your provision, I want you; more than your gifts, I want you; more than your blessing, I want you. I will stay here with these grumbling, idolatrous Israelites who break my heart and bring me so much pain if only I can be with you."

Before having a personal relationship with God, we do not understand how the presence of God can be so important that it outweighs every other blessing in life. We cannot comprehend how the psalmist could sing to God, "Better is one day in your courts / than a thousand elsewhere" (Psalm 84:10) or why David would write, "One thing I ask from the LORD, / this only do I seek: / that I may dwell in the house of the LORD / all the days of my life, / to gaze on the beauty of the LORD / and to seek him in his temple" (Psalm 27:4). But once we come to know God in a personal way, we begin to understand what David was singing about. When we have experienced the depth of love, comfort, and encouragement that comes from being in the presence of God, we want to hold on to it forever.

Often it's when we are in the wilderness that we have the most difficult time experiencing the fullness of God's presence, yet this is when we need to feel his presence most. Sometimes the presence of God comes upon us suddenly and unexpectedly—such as in a still small voice, as "deep calls to deep" (Psalm 42:7), or as a mighty wave that rushes over us. But there are other times when we must purposefully seek God and his presence as Moses did. This can mean setting aside particular times to be alone with God as well as changing up your normal devotional time. Pray and read the Bible out loud. Write down your prayers. Sing a hymn. Kneel or raise your hands when you pray. Memorize a verse of Scripture and let it be your prayer guide for the week. Go somewhere that brings life into your spirit—a trail you enjoy walking, a beautiful park, or a beach if one is close enough. Find some place that reminds you of the goodness of God and puts you at peace with yourself.

For the Israelites, later known as the Jews, the city of Jerusalem was the place where they felt most connected to God. Referred to as the City of David, the City of Peace, and the Holy City, it was more than the seat of political and economic power; it was the place where the Temple was located. Within the Temple—just as there had been in the Tabernacle as the Israelites wandered in the wilderness— there was an inner sanctum known as the Holy of Holies where the Jews believed the manifest presence of God dwelled on earth. It was considered to be so holy that only one man, the high priest, could enter there—and only on one day of the year for one purpose: to make atonement for the sins of the people. Observant Jews would travel to Jerusalem three times each year for religious festivals where they would be close to God. To be in Jerusalem was in some real, almost mystical way to be where God's presence dwelled.

Even today Jews around the world end the two holiest days of the year—the Day of Atonement and the last day of Passover—by saying, "Next year in Jerusalem." Those words are spoken as a hope and a promise, meaning that even if one is not in Jerusalem physically, he or she will be there spiritually and will be closer to where God is this time next year.

Years ago when I was in Jerusalem, a rabbi was asked to explain to our group the importance of Jerusalem to the Jews. When he spoke to us, the Soviet Union was still intact and was persecuting people of faith. This rabbi often traveled there and held secret meetings with Jews, worshiping with them and teaching them from the Scriptures. As the years progressed, he came to look forward to those trips because of the great joy he experienced in reconnecting with people he had come to know and love. But often they were times of sorrow because it was not uncommon for one or two people to be missing, having been arrested by the government and sentenced to three or more years in an insane asylum or the mines in Siberia.

On one trip, a young man who had become particularly dear to the rabbi was missing. This young man had been arrested and found guilty of crimes against the government. Before his sentence was imposed, the court asked if he would like to make a statement. The rabbi told us that the brave young man said this: "I would. My statement is this. You may imprison my body, but my spirit is free. For my soul is a citizen of another country, and I answer to a court much higher than yours." He then looked at those who had judged him and added the words he knew would cost him: "Next year in Jerusalem!" Those words did cost him, adding six more months of labor in the tundra of Siberia.

The rabbi was stunned three and a half years later when he received a phone call from the young man, who was calling from the Bucharest airport. He said, "I'm free. I'm coming. Get a car. Meet me at the airport. No friends, no fanfare. Just pick me up and drive me to the Wailing Wall. All my life I have said, 'Next year in Jerusalem.' This is the year!"

Sometimes seeking God's
presence requires more than
setting aside a time and place
to be alone with him;
it requires us to work diligently
to clear our hearts of all the attitudes
and emotions that impede us from
experiencing the presence of God.

The rabbi then looked at us and said, "Do not underestimate the power of this city. There are people who would give their lives to be where you are. There are people around the world who would die to be where you are. Don't miss this."

If God dwelt in some faraway city and we could travel there to be in his presence, every one of us would go. We would change our plans, clear our calendars, and make whatever sacrifices were required. We would go and be with him. And we would make certain that our hearts were ready to encounter him. We would look within and remove all that would keep us from experiencing his presence in its fullness.

Of course, we know that we do not need to travel anywhere to experience God's presence. The Bible tells us that Christ makes his home in our very hearts. We do, however, need to make certain that our hearts are right if we are to feel the fullness of his presence. Sometimes seeking God's presence requires more than setting aside a time and place to be alone with him; it requires us to work diligently to clear our hearts of all the attitudes and emotions that impede us from experiencing the presence of God—including anger, bitterness, envy, greed, self-pity, self-centeredness, and unforgiveness, to name just a few. Sadly, these attitudes that make it hard for us to experience the presence of God are the very ones that the wilderness so often creates within us. So, when we feel devastated by the circumstances of our lives, it's more important than ever to look within and pray as David did: "Create in me a clean heart, O God, / and put a new and right spirit within me" (Psalm 51:10 NRSV). Here we find David praying for a right spirit within himself, but first he acknowledges the wrongness of his heart and the sins he has committed. He looks within himself and is honest about what he finds there.

I often have told people that they cannot give to God what they do not have. What I mean is that before God cleanses our hearts, we must "own" what we find there. We must admit to ourselves and to God whatever we find within us that inhibits us from experiencing the fullness of his presence. "Owning" the ugliness within ourselves means we don't blame it on our circumstances or other people. We accept responsibility for what we have allowed to fill our hearts.

Once we do that, it's ours. We "have" it, and we can give it to God by asking him to take it from us, forgive us, cleanse us, and make our hearts a fitting place for his presence to dwell. In some ways this journey within is much more difficult and threatening than traveling to a distant city. But it is essential for everyone who wants to walk in God's presence.

In addition to being alone with God and following David's example of examining our hearts and asking God to cleanse us, there are other ways we can be intentional in seeking God's presence in the wilderness. I encourage you to be consistent in reading the Bible, participating in corporate worship, and serving others. Whether you feel anything or not, continue these habits. Open your life to God's presence, and you will experience him. Like water to a thirsty soul in the desert, the presence of God will bring you life in the wilderness.

Maya Angelou, a great American poet and author, made an incredible statement about the presence of God in our lives. She wrote, "Of all the needs...a lonely child has, the one that must be satisfied if there is going to be hope and a hope of wholeness is the unshaking need for an unshakable God."[1] My guess is that she may have been writing from her own experiences as a child. When she was seven years old, she was raped. When she told what had happened to her, her family was furious; but the legal system did nothing. Shortly after it became apparent that her rapist would go free, he was brutally murdered. Angelou was traumatized both by what had been done to her and by the thought that her words had caused the death of this man. For the next five years, she didn't speak another word. My heart breaks to think about the wilderness in which this poor child lived. But my heart rejoices that an unwavering God who cares about those who suffer set her caged spirit free, and how she did sing!

In the wilderness, everything shakes. Nothing is steady. Even the ground you're standing upon feels like it is about to give way. The one and only thing that is true and unshakable is God. Seek his presence when you are in the wilderness, and you will find—as Maya Angelou and countless others have—that his promise is true:

Do not fear, for I am with you;
    do not be afraid, for I am your God;
I will strengthen you, I will help you,
    I will uphold you with my victorious right hand.
                    (Isaiah 41:10 NRSV)

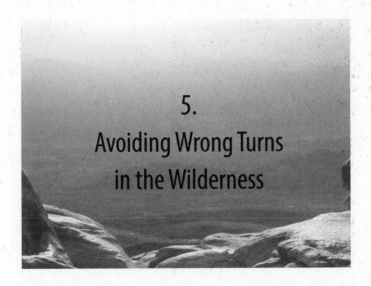

5.
Avoiding Wrong Turns
in the Wilderness

5.
Avoiding Wrong Turns in the Wilderness

It was October 25, 1964, and Jim Marshall was having a great day on the football field. His Minnesota Vikings were defeating the San Francisco 49ers.

Marshall played defensive end for the Vikings, a position he held from 1961 to 1979. He was the heart and soul of "The Purple People Eaters," ranked by ESPN as one of the top five defensive ends of all time. He started 270 consecutive games—a record that stood for thirty years—and played in four Super Bowls. He recovered more opponents' fumbles than anyone in NFL history, and if the league had kept statistics for sacks when he played, Marshall would be among the leaders. To this day he is known as the NFL's Iron Man. His jersey is on display at the Hall of Fame in Canton, Ohio. But unlike two of his defensive line teammates, Carl Eller and Alan Page, Marshall has never been voted into the Hall of Fame. Perhaps it has something to do with what happened during the game on that fateful day in October.

Marshall had already caused the 49er quarterback, George Myra, to fumble. Eller had picked it up and run it in for a touchdown. Now it was Marshall's turn. Myra dropped back to pass, evaded the Viking rush, and completed a pass to Billy Kilmer, who fumbled when he was hit. Marshall scooped up the ball and ran sixty-six yards into the end zone—the wrong end zone. Teammates ran after him, yelling for him to stop. His coaches on the sidelines frantically tried to wave him off. All to no avail. Marshall's first thought that something had gone wrong was when he was given a hug in the end zone by a 49er. Along with his other accomplishments, Marshall holds the record for the shortest play in NFL history—minus sixty-six yards.

Most commentators believe Marshall had a Hall of Fame career, and most believe that he's not in the Hall because of that one play that will forever be associated with him. It's possible to take one wrong turn on the football field and never make it into the Hall of Fame. Likewise, it's possible to take one wrong turn in the wilderness and never get to the Promised Land God has waiting for us.

We've said that the wilderness is a time when we are overwhelmed, tested, and tempted by the circumstances of our lives. Often our hearts are heavy, our spirits are dry, and we wonder how we'll get through the rest of the day, much less the rest of our lives. But the wilderness is also a time of enormous opportunities. Brought to our knees by the problems we are facing, there is the very real possibility that we will learn to trust God in a deeper way, grow closer to him than ever before, and be transformed into the image of Christ. In order for that to happen, we must avoid some wrong turns in the wilderness—wrong turns that, as the Israelites show us, are very easy to make.

After Moses delivered the Israelites from slavery in Egypt and received the Law at Mount Sinai, he led them into the wilderness on their way to the Promised Land. We have seen that there are times when we enter a wilderness because of our wrong decisions or the devastating acts of others, but this time the wilderness was God's plan for Israel. He led them into the wilderness as a necessary part of the journey that would bring them to the future blessings he had prepared for them. It was a journey that should have taken only a few months. Instead, the Israelites spent forty years there—making it the longest wilderness experience recorded in the Bible. Why? Because they took some wrong turns—not geographically, but spiritually. With their attitudes and their behaviors, they turned away from God and the lessons he wanted to teach them. As a result, instead of spending a relatively short time in the difficult terrain of the wilderness, they spent four decades there. Most of those who left Egypt never entered the Promised Land God had waiting for them.

When we're in a wilderness period, the same wrong turns that diverted the Israelites are waiting for us as well. If we take them, they will turn us around and send us even farther into the wilderness, causing us to be there much longer than necessary. Let's take a careful look at three wrong turns the Israelites made and learn how we can avoid these unnecessary wilderness detours.

Turning Our Mouths Against God

If we are to navigate our wilderness experiences well, we need to avoid the temptation of turning our mouths against God. The Israelites complained against Moses and God constantly for forty years. Read their story in the books of Exodus and Numbers, and you will be amazed by how often you come across phrases such as "but the Israelites grumbled," "the children of Israel complained," and "Israel argued."

It started just as soon as they left Egypt. Moses told Pharaoh to let his people go, and Pharaoh refused. The Israelites were his slave labor force. Much of Egypt's wealth depended on the cheap labor they provided. Losing them would be disastrous to his nation's economy and to his reign. So God brought judgment upon Egypt in the form of various plagues. Finally, when Pharaoh could stand it no more, he relented and allowed the Israelites to leave.

After a short time, Pharaoh had second thoughts. He sent his army to find the Israelites and bring them back. As Pharaoh's forces drew closer, the Israelites saw them approaching in the distance. What did they do? Did they pray? Did they get their heads together and figure out a plan? Did they look each other in the eyes and say, "Time to man up and fight for our freedom"? No, they went to Moses, not to pledge their loyalty—not to say, "You're the leader, the one God speaks to; tell us what to do, and we'll stand with you"—but to complain and attack. They lamented, "Was it because there were no graves in Egypt that you brought us to the desert to die? What have you done to us by bringing us out of Egypt? Didn't we say to you in Egypt, 'Leave us alone; let us serve the Egyptians'? It would have been better for us to serve the Egyptians than to die in the desert!" (Exodus 14:11-12).

Here's my translation: "What, Moses? You couldn't kill us in Egypt? You had to drag us out here to do it? We were doing fine before you came into our lives and started talking about freedom and a Promised Land. We liked being slaves. It's all we've ever known. We come from a long line of slaves, and no one ever complained." (Of course, they always complained.) "You and your talk about freedom are going to get us killed."

Moses responded by turning away from them and toward God. He asked God for the plan, God gave it to him, and he obeyed. As Moses raised his staff, the sea parted; and they walked through the waters—the Bible says "as if on dry ground." The Egyptians came roaring toward them, but the waters crashed down upon them. So the armies of Pharaoh were destroyed, and the people of Israel were saved.

I can imagine the Israelites looking at each other and asking, "Did you see that? Did you know that God could do that, because frankly, I didn't know that God could do that. If I had known that God could do that, I never would have complained, not even a little. Now that I know what God can do, you'll never hear me complain again. I promise."

They didn't complain again—for three whole days. First they said, "We don't have any water to drink, Moses." Then they said, "We don't have any food to eat, Moses." Next it was, "Moses, we don't like the food we've been given." Later they grumbled, "Moses, you and your family get to work in the tabernacle, but you won't allow our families to work in the tabernacle. Why do you get to do it? It's not fair. God's not fair. Life's not fair. Life's too hard. We don't like this wilderness thing." And on and on it went for forty years.

You know people like that, don't you? They love to complain. They wouldn't have a reason to get up in the morning if they didn't have something to complain about. I've heard it said that if they had been present when Jesus fed the five thousand with two fish and five loaves of bread, they would have complained that there was no lemon for the fish and no butter for the bread. Somehow it makes them feel like everything's right in the world if they can point out something that's wrong.

When we get into that place of
self-pity where we are
complaining and grumbling,
very often what's beneath our
words is anger with God
for allowing us to go through
the very trials we need in
order to become more like Jesus.

That's how it was with the Israelites. They constantly went against Moses with ridicule, sarcasm, criticism, and complaints. Eventually, their anger escalated into threats against his leadership and even his life. When Moses had had enough, he told them to stop, warning them that their words were more serious than they realized. He said, "Who are we, that you should grumble against us?...You are not grumbling against us, but against the LORD" (Exodus 16:7-8).

Moses was essentially saying to the Israelites, "This wilderness thing that you're not so sold on—it's not my thing for you; it's God's thing for you. This freedom idea that you don't want any part of—I didn't dream it up for you; it's God's plan for you. You think you're complaining against me, but you're actually grumbling against God. You're not attacking me; you're rebelling against God. So you had better be very careful with the words you speak."

We're often guilty of the same thing. We'd never admit that we're grumbling against God or complaining about his will for our lives, and yet that is exactly what we're doing. With our complaints, we are saying to God, "I shouldn't have it so hard. I shouldn't have to endure all these problems. I'm trying to be faithful, and still I have all these troubles in my life. I don't deserve this." Whether we will acknowledge it or not, our grumbling is saying, "God, you should take better care of me. I'm trying to do your will, and, frankly, God, I deserve better. Start doing your job and get me out of this." We'd never put it that way. But when we get into that place of self-pity where we are complaining and grumbling, very often what's beneath our words is anger with God for allowing us to go through the very trials we need in order to become more like Jesus.

Of course, it is never wrong to be honest about how we feel—to be transparent with God and with others about our problems. As we've seen, admitting how hard life is and how much pain we're experiencing is critical when we are in the wilderness. That's how we gain wisdom and receive guidance. Telling God and others that our path is difficult and our strength seems insufficient is a humble admission of our need for help, and that is to be encouraged. After all, Jesus said, "Blessed are the poor in spirit, for theirs is the kingdom of heaven" (Matthew 5:3).

There's a popular view that teaches if you want to be spiritual, you should ignore your problems, act like they're not real, and keep making positive confessions about your situation; the promised result is that you will rise above the negative events in your life, untouched by the problems and the pain of the world. That's simply not true, and that's not what it means to be spiritual. Being spiritual means looking at your life in an honest way, acknowledging your problems as well as your joys, and then bringing them to God so that he can work powerfully in your life.

As I mentioned in the previous chapter, before we can give God our problems, we must "have" them—acknowledge them, understand them, and own whatever we may have done to create them. Bringing our problems to others who can help us understand what is going on in our lives, encourage us, and pray for us prepares us to give our problems to God. But when telling others about our problems, we must be careful that we are truly seeking insight and guidance, not merely wanting to vent against God or grumble about how difficult our life is.

Likewise, when we pray about our problems, our intent should be to bear our lives transparently before God, asking for guidance and strength. I love people who are absolutely honest with God. Their prayers are real and sometimes raw. They pour out their pain and frustration to God with deep emotion. I love it because it's authentic and because it's how the psalmists so often prayed. They spoke to God about their suffering and their confusion and even at times about how they felt abandoned by God. But they didn't stay there. Read the psalms and you'll find that the ones referred to as "laments," in which the psalmist cries out about his problems, most often end with the psalmist remembering how God has been faithful in the past and declaring that he will trust God for the future. I encourage you to pour out your heart to God, holding nothing back. Honesty, even when it's raw and emotional, brings our lives before God.

Complaining and grumbling are different. They don't open our lives to God; they set our lives against God. It's good and healthy to be real and emotional as we pray to God from the wilderness. But even in the wilderness, we can remember that God is faithful and be grateful for his promises. And in those moments God will give us strength.

Some time ago I conducted a funeral for a woman in our church whom my wife and I had known for many years. Her name was Kathleen, and she was an incredible woman. Twenty years previously she and her husband, Jim, left their lucrative medical careers—he was a doctor, and she was a nurse—when Kathleen felt called to begin a mission that would take medical care to the most dangerous and remote locations in Guatemala. When she first shared this idea with her husband, he said, "Sweetheart, that's crazy. Genocide is going on there. It's happening right where you want to go. People are being killed there for no good reason. It's just too dangerous." She told him, "I'm going. God put it on my heart. You can go or not go. But I'm going."

So they sold their two Mercedes and their beautiful home on the lake, and they purchased the supplies they would need to do the work Kathleen felt God had called her to do. They left all that was familiar, and they began a mission that has provided medical care for tens of thousands of people. Some of the poorest people in the Western Hemisphere who never had seen a doctor received the medical care they needed because Kathleen stepped out in faith and obeyed God. They partnered with pastors in Guatemala so that the gospel was always shared wherever they went. As a result, thousands of people came to faith in Christ and hundreds of churches were started.

After twelve years of serving the poor in Guatemala, Kathleen was diagnosed with cancer, and soon the prognosis was very grim. A well-meaning friend came to her and said, "I know God will heal you. He has to heal you. He owes it to you." Kathleen, already in great pain, looked at her friend and said, "God doesn't owe me anything. I owe him everything." Even in her darkest moments, when it would have been easy to say, "I deserve better," she remembered all that God had done for her. In a wilderness of suffering and with death approaching, Kathleen did not complain that she deserved better. Instead, what flowed from her heart was gratitude for God's faithfulness and care.

God had been faithful to the Israelites as well. He had delivered them from slavery and miraculously provided for their needs again and again. They had many reasons to be thankful. Yet whenever a new problem arose, instead of remembering God's provision and being grateful, they grumbled and complained. Finally God had enough. He told the Israelites that he would not allow them to enter the Promised Land but would send them back into the wilderness where he would teach them and prepare the next generation for the future he had for them. Other than Joshua and Caleb, none of the generation that left Egypt would enter the Promised Land and experience the life of promise that God had planned for them.

Can a grumbling mouth and a complaining spirit actually keep us from the life God has for us? Absolutely, because they reveal a hardened heart. And when your heart is hard, you cannot receive the grace or learn the lessons that you need in order to leave the wilderness and step into the land of promise.

The wilderness, by definition, is incredibly difficult and terribly painful. You will need to talk to God and to others about what you're going through. But be careful that you do not develop a grumbling spirit or a complaining heart. Use your words to bring your needs and questions to God, not to set your life against God.

Turning Our Ears to the Wrong People

Another mistake we will be tempted to make in the wilderness is turning our ears to the wrong people. One of the reasons the Israelites grumbled and complained so often is that they listened to the wrong advice.

When the children of Israel began to complain that they didn't have enough food in the wilderness, God promised to provide "bread from heaven." They woke up the next morning, and all over the ground was something they had never seen. It was white and looked like frost, but it tasted like wafers with honey. The Israelites looked at each other and said, "What is it?" (Exodus 16:15). So they called it *manna*, which means literally "What is it?"[1] They could hardly believe what God had done for them.

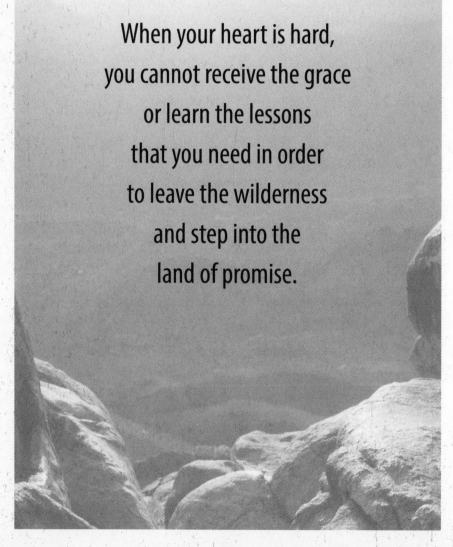

When your heart is hard,
you cannot receive the grace
or learn the lessons
that you need in order
to leave the wilderness
and step into the
land of promise.

For the people of Israel, manna in the wilderness wasn't merely nourishment. It was a sign of God's grace. It spoke of God's commitment to them, promising that God knew their needs and would continue to provide what they needed. They wanted as much of this gift as they could hold on to, but God told them to take only what they needed for a single day. Manna didn't have a long shelf life. It would spoil overnight, so they were to gather only as much as they needed for that day. The promise was that God would provide what they needed each day.

God was providing for the needs of his people on a deeper level than they understood. He was teaching them the spiritual lesson that he could be trusted. Daily. He wanted them to learn to trust the Provider, not the provision—the Giver, not the gift. In essence, he was teaching the Israelites how to walk with him in faith.

It's understandable that some of the Israelites did not follow instructions that first day. What God had provided was incredible—better than they had expected. Not only did the manna meet their physical needs, but it also represented God's presence and his compassion for them. So they eagerly gathered what they needed, but some of them kept part of it until morning. What God had done for them was so amazing and generous that they wanted to be sure they would have it the next day. It was as if they wanted to get their arms around it and hold on to it, ensuring it would be theirs forever.

Now here's what interesting. Later the Israelites would come to hate this marvelous gift they once treasured. They would despise it, complaining that what God had given them was no longer good enough—that he shouldn't expect them to be satisfied with this manna. How did they go from gratitude to grumbling? They listened to the wrong people.

When the Israelites left Egypt, others left with them who were not Israelites but who also had been mistreated and oppressed by the Egyptians. When they saw the Israelites making their exodus, they decided it was a chance for them to escape as well. No one was standing at the gates checking papers to determine who was an Israelite and who wasn't, so they stepped into the mass of people who were leaving and escaped. The Bible refers to these people as "the rabble." They did not worship the God of Israel, and they did not want to learn his ways or follow his laws. But they traveled and camped with the Israelites. In Numbers 11 we read, "The rabble with them began to crave other food, and again the Israelites started wailing and said, 'If only we had meat to eat!...We never see anything but this manna!'" (verses 4, 6). Did you see how this complaining started? The Israelites turned their ears to the wrong people, and once again they became dissatisfied with what God had done for them.

Do you remember when God's grace became real to you for the first time? It was like a magnificent gift you never expected. It was so good, so unlike anything you had ever known, so much more than you knew you deserved that you wondered, *What is this that has changed the way I think, the way I feel, the way I want to live? Whatever it is, I want to get my arms around it and hold on to it for the rest of my life.*

Maybe this grace came to you when, like Israel, you were in slavery and bondage. Perhaps what held you captive was a drink, a drug, or some self-destructive pattern in your life. You thought, "I'll never be free of this. I'll never enter a land of promise." But then Jesus Christ came into your life, and everything changed. You were set free, and your desires began to change. God did for you what you could not do for yourself: you were free from what had enslaved you, and you were alive inside. When you realized what had saved you was the grace of God, you wanted to put your arms around it and hold on. You thought to yourself, *I never want to let this go. I'll never need anything else as long as I know that God is with me.*

Or maybe your experience of God's love was different. Maybe you were "the good kid." You did everything right and worked hard to prove yourself. You were going to achieve enough so that people would accept you and love you. But no matter how much you did and how much people praised you, it was never enough because your struggle wasn't about getting other people to love you; it was about being able to love and accept yourself. Even deeper than that, your struggle was to do enough so that you could be certain God would see you and accept you. Having to perform and measure up and labor for approval finally became a heavy yoke around your neck. But then the grace of Jesus Christ came into your life, and that yoke was broken. Everything changed for you. No longer did you feel like a slave trying to do enough for your master, but you felt like a son or a daughter who was accepted by a loving Father. When that gift came into your life, it was everything you wanted and more. You thought, *If only I can get my arms around this gift and hold on to it forever, I'll never need anything else.*

Perhaps your story was different than either of these scenarios. Maybe you spent your life seeking the things the world said would make you happy, but after trading your life for money and possessions and success, you felt empty inside. What the world told you was everything left you feeling like nothing—discontent, disappointed, and dead inside. But then Jesus Christ stepped into your life, and for the first time you were at peace. You felt right inside, and it was so unexpected and marvelous that you thought, *If only I can hold on to Jesus, I will never need anything else.*

Do you remember the first time you saw Jesus for who he was? You saw the purity of his heart as he died for your sins on the cross. You saw his blood flowing and washing away those sins. You found yourself able to stand in front of a holy God as an accepted, loved, and free son or daughter because of Jesus. You wanted to embrace that moment and hold on to it forever. Every new truth you learned was a treasure. Every new day was an adventure. Every moment was an opportunity to know God and share his love with others. And you told yourself, *If I have nothing else in life, this will be enough.*

That's where I believe the Israelites may have been before the rabble began to speak to them. Imagine the conversation with me.

"Hey, don't get me wrong. I like manna as much as the next guy, but is this all your God is ever going to give you? I mean, you're going through such a hard time here in the wilderness. It just seems like he could give you something different every now and then."

"What's wrong with this manna?"

"Nothing's wrong with it, but I was just thinking about back in the day, when we were living the life in Egypt. I know we were slaves, but do you remember the food there and how good it was? Do you remember the meat? I can almost taste it now. I'm just wondering why your new master isn't as good to you as your old master—why he doesn't give you the same things you once had?"

I have learned that when we are in the wilderness, the rabble will come. Though some people will come to you because they love you, see you struggling, and want to help you, many others will come who will be like the rabble in the wilderness. They will not know God or his grace or what is required to walk faithfully with him. Like the rabble, they may be camping with you. They may be members of your family or friends who care for you, or even members of your church who haven't progressed in their faith. And this is what they will say:

> Feeling dissatisfied in your marriage is more than you should have to endure. You shouldn't have to struggle so much to have a marriage that is good. You can't forgive how you've been hurt. There's a way out, and you should take it.

> Being a teenager is hard—not fitting in, feeling like you don't belong. Take this. Drink this. Hang out with us. There's an easy way out of this wilderness.

> Standing up for your faith only makes others look down on you, push you away, and leave you out. Just keep your mouth shut. Go with the flow.

> Look, you shouldn't have to go through (*insert your own wilderness*). You deserve better. God should provide more for you than this. He should change your circumstances and give you an easy way out of this wilderness. If he loved you, he would.

I also have learned that if the rabble does not come to us when we're struggling, very often we are tempted to go to them. When we are in the wilderness and there is no end in sight, we are tempted to find someone who went through the very thing we're facing and took the easy way out. We may not know it at the time, but when we do that, we're looking for someone who will give us permission to take the easy way too.

The conversation goes something like this: "Hey, I just want to learn a little bit, you know. I'm going through this difficult time. I think you went through it too. And you seem to be at a much better place. What did you do?" After telling you what he or she did, the person will say, "Oh, by the way, it's the best decision I ever made. I can't tell you how much better my life is now. I thought it was going to be hard. But I did it, and now my life is great and I'm so happy."

For God's sake and yours, do not listen to the rabble when you're in the wilderness. Even if they care about you, do not listen to their advice when they come to you. And don't seek them out. Find someone who walked through the wilderness you're in but did it God's way. Find someone who walked through it the hard and costly way. Ask this person what he or she did, and you'll hear something like this: "It was the hardest thing I ever did, but it was the most important thing I ever did. It made me who I am today. It drew me closer to God, and it allowed me to look myself in the mirror and be proud of the person I see."

I have learned that the right way out of the wilderness is never the easy way. Real growth is hard and painful. Being transformed into the image of Jesus requires sacrifice, self-denial, and bearing a cross. There may be shortcuts to happiness, but there are no shortcuts to holiness. There are times in life when we must bear what seems unbearable and persevere when our strength seems gone.

But know this: Your pain is not meant to last forever. The Israelites remained in the wilderness for forty years only because they refused to learn the lessons God had to teach them. They would have been out of the desert and into the Promised Land in just a few months if their hearts had remained open to God. Instead, they listened to the wrong people, became dissatisfied with what God had done for them, and allowed their hearts to go from gratitude to grumbling.

Don't forget what God has done for you. Don't forget where you were when he delivered you from bondage. Don't forget how precious his grace once was to you—how you knew that if all you had was God, you had enough. Don't listen to the rabble. Seek out those who went through the wilderness the right way, not the easy way. And ask God for the wisdom and grace to persevere.

Turning Our Eyes Away from God

A third temptation we face in the wilderness is turning our eyes away from God. More than anything else, what kept the Israelites out of the Promised Land was their habit of continually focusing on their problems rather than looking to God. They did this many times during their wilderness wanderings, but perhaps the most egregious occasion was when they came to the border of the Promised Land the first time. As we've already seen, God told them to go in and conquer the land, and Moses sent in twelve trusted men to spy out the land. They came back with two very different reports. The majority report, supported by ten of the twelve, acknowledged that the land was fertile and productive. But then they very quickly told their fellow Israelites,

> "The people who live there are powerful, and the cities are fortified and very large. We even saw descendants of Anak there.... We can't attack those people; they are stronger than we are.... All the people we saw there are of great size. We saw the Nephilim there (the descendants of Anak come from the Nephilim). We seemed like grasshoppers in our own eyes, and we looked the same to them" (Numbers 13:28, 31-33).

In effect they were saying, "We've never seen anything like it. If you had seen what we saw, you would know there's no way we could take them. You'd know that the only thing we can do is go back through the wilderness to Egypt and ask Pharaoh to take us back."

We've also seen that the other two spies, Caleb and Joshua, saw the same things but came back with a very different report: "The land we passed through and explored is exceedingly good. If the LORD is pleased with us, he will lead us into that land, a land flowing with milk and honey, and will give it to us. Only do not rebel against the LORD. And do not be afraid of the people of the land, because we will devour them. Their protection is gone, but the LORD is with us. Do not be afraid of them" (Numbers 14:7-9).

Caleb and Joshua saw the same people, the same cities, and the same fortifications as the other ten, but they looked to see something else. They looked to see where God was, what God was doing, and what God had promised. And they saw that God was with them. Instead of seeing a Problem Land, they saw a Promised Land. So they urged the people to step forward in faith and trust God to keep his promises to them.

How big were the people in the Promised Land? I don't have a clue. But I know this: any time we focus on a problem, it seems huge. And that's what we often do. When we have a problem or face a challenge, we take it out, hold it up, and look at it closer and closer until it's all we can see. At that point, it is absolutely mammoth in size.

Where you direct the eyes of your heart will determine what you believe to be true, what choices you will make, and whether you will live in faith or fear. There are many things in life you can't control. You can't control your spouse. After they reach a certain age, you can't control your children. You can't even control your cat. You can't control cancer. You can't control the drunk driver in the lane next to you. You can't control whether people like you. You can't control the stock market or the economy. Most things in life you cannot control at all. But you can always control what is most important in life, and that is where you choose to focus the spiritual eyes of your heart. Focus on your problems, looking at them over and over, and they will seem huge; and you will come to believe that you can never overcome them. Focus on your inabilities, and you will be limited by all the things you cannot do. Even if you focus on your abilities, you will be limited to what you can do. But if you will focus on God, you will be limited only by what God can do through you. And that's not bad! As the Apostle Paul wrote, "I can do all things through him who strengthens me" (Philippians 4:13 NRSV).

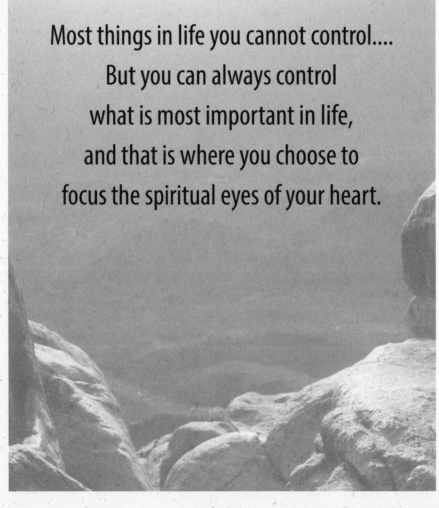

Most things in life you cannot control....
But you can always control
what is most important in life,
and that is where you choose to
focus the spiritual eyes of your heart.

More important than what happens *to* you is what happens *in* you; and when you focus on God, good things happen *in* you: faith, strength, vision, confidence—everything you need to step into the promises of God and overcome the obstacles before you.

Loreine Johnston was a beautiful example of this truth. I remember the day that she motioned for me to follow her out of her husband Billy's hospital room into the hallway. The doctors had predicted that Billy's long bout with cancer would be over in just a week. Her own fight with cancer was just beginning. She had been diagnosed a month previously.

Through the many years of Billy's treatment, Loreine had felt it so important to be strong for him. And she had been. Even in the last month, she had never told him about her diagnosis. She didn't want to worry him, so he would die without ever knowing.

Loreine had seen what cancer could do; now she would face it herself. As we stood in the hall so that Billy couldn't hear, she told me that it seemed too much to bear. Her best friend and the love of her life soon would be gone. She felt all alone and didn't know how she would make it.

Then she handed me a sympathy card she had been holding and asked me to read it. Inside a friend had written a little note; it said: *You will never know that Jesus is all you need until Jesus is all you have.*

As I gave the card back to her, she looked at me through tears and said, "I'm praying that card is right, because that's where I am."

I visited Loreine in her home during her treatments after Billy's death. Some women from the church did as well. Two of them came to see me after one of their visits. They struggled for words as if they didn't know what to say. Then one of them spoke up: "Rob, we're not sure what to do with this, but we almost feel guilty when we visit Loreine. She's dying of cancer, but when we leave her house, we feel happy and comforted. It doesn't seem right."

I knew what they meant. I had had the same experience. At first when I went to see Loreine, I struggled with what I would say to bring her comfort. I would pray for God to give me words that might cheer her up and give her strength. The first visits were tough. When I had visited before, Billy had been there. But now he was gone.

And there was no getting around the reality of her own impending death. She was depressed, and I would leave taking the heaviness of the room with me.

Then something changed. I'm not certain I recognized it the first time it happened. But just like the women who came to see me, I began to leave Loreine's home filled with joy. It didn't seem right. I told myself not to feel that way, but there was such peace and strength within her that I couldn't help myself.

On one visit, I asked, "Loreine, you don't seem frightened anymore or overwhelmed. What's going on?"

Her answer was as profound as it was simple. This is what she said:

> Rob, God is with me. I started praying like I have never prayed before. I decided I wanted him to be the center of my life—not my cancer or my loneliness. So I took to heart the verse, "Seek the LORD while he may be found" (Isaiah 55:6). And I have found him—or he has found me. I don't know which. But when I'm in my room at night, while I'm in bed and praying, God's presence is so powerful and so real that some nights I'm afraid to open my eyes because it feels like I will be looking him in the face. Jesus is all I've got, but now I know he's all I need.

As Loreine discovered, there is a truth greater than cancer. There is a truth greater than your pain. There is a truth greater than your loss and greater than your fears. There is a truth greater than the wilderness that says you're all alone and there's no hope. It's the truth that God is with you.

Let the world take your health. Let it take your finances. Let it take all that was rightfully yours and everything you had planned. Let it take you into a wilderness that you can't make sense of or find a way out of on your own. But don't ever let it take your eyes off of God and his promises. Never allow this world and your problems to take from you the assurance that God is with you. Remember his promise, "I will never leave you or forsake you" (Hebrews 13:5 NRSV).

Your wilderness will be a painful time. It will be full of problems that seem bigger than you are and beyond your ability to cope. And if you focus on them, you will lose heart and give up. But remember what Jesus said the night before his death: "In this world you will have trouble. But take heart! I have overcome the world" (John 16:33). This is a promise to hold on to. Take heart, the One who overcame the world and its troubles has promised to be with you. Look for him, and you will find him.

Focus on your problems, look at your limitations, become fixated on how far you have to go, or worry about everything that could go wrong, and your challenges will appear to be giants. You will feel as small as a grasshopper. But if you will look to the God of the universe; if you will seek the One who lived in the same world you do and overcame its troubles; if you will turn your eyes to the God who loves you and has promised a future of blessing for you—in his presence your problems will no longer seem so large. You will walk through your wilderness with a strength that is not your own. You will discover that when Jesus is all you have, Jesus is all you need.

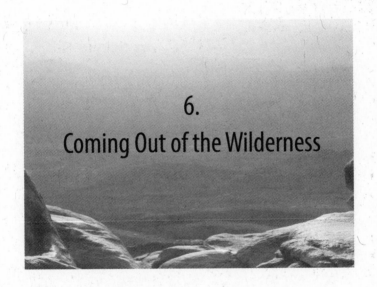

6.
Coming Out of the Wilderness

6.
Coming Out of the Wilderness

In Chapter 3 of the Book of Hebrews, the author describes the rebellion and unbelief of the Israelites that kept them from entering the Promised Land. The fourth chapter begins with this admonition to readers: "Therefore, since the promise of entering his rest still stands, let us be careful that none of you be found to have fallen short of it" (Hebrews 4:1).

The warning in this verse is important, and we need to hear it. We can fall short of what God desires, never learning the lessons of the wilderness and never coming out of it.

But before we are given the warning, we are given a word of assurance and encouragement: "Since the promise of entering his rest still stands." God has a place ready for us where we will rest from the struggles of the wilderness. There is a land of promise for us where we will experience the peace and the abundance of God's blessing. God does not want us to stay in the wilderness forever. His desire is that we come out of the wilderness, step into his rest, and live in his promises.

Let me share with you three "parting" thoughts about the benefits of the wilderness that will serve you well as you leave it behind and step into the rest that God has for you.

1. The Wilderness Will Reveal Your Heart

The wilderness is a period of great stress—spiritually, emotionally, and sometimes relationally and physically. The wilderness puts pressure on us like no other time in our lives. And one thing pressure always does is reveal who we truly are.

At one of the churches I served when I was a young pastor, we always had a children's sermon. One Sunday morning I had three bowls, each one holding a large sponge. I told the kids, "All of these sponges look the same. But I soaked one in water, one in milk, and one in cooking oil. How can we find out what's inside each one?"

It was an easy question, and the children had no trouble coming up with the answer. In unison they cried out, "Squeeze them."

Put the squeeze on something and, if you do it with enough pressure, what's inside will come flowing out. That's what the wilderness does to us. It puts the squeeze on us. It brings great pressure and stress into our lives. But as painful as that may be, it's only under pressure that we discover who we are on the inside.

From time to time your doctor may prescribe a stress test. He or she will listen to your heart and run an EKG. But if there are any real concerns, your doctor is likely to order a stress test to see how your heart performs under pressure. Why? Because under pressure the true condition of your heart will be revealed.

The wilderness is a spiritual stress test. It shows us the real condition of our spiritual hearts, our character, and our faith. When everything is going well, we can fool ourselves. When life is easy, we can believe that we are further along in our relationship with God than we truly are. When we're not being tested, we can believe that our inner, moral core is stronger than it is. But when the wilderness puts the squeeze on us, there's just no hiding what's inside of us; it comes flowing out of us. That's what we saw with the Israelites. When life became difficult, they responded with fear, unbelief, and criticism. Why? Because that's who they were inside.

Sometimes when we see someone we admire make an awful mistake, we say, "That was so out of character." It may not be the way that person normally acts, but it wasn't out of character. Every decision we make, good or bad, flows out of our character. Remember what Jesus taught: "For out of the heart come evil thoughts—murder, adultery, sexual immorality, theft, false testimony, slander" (Matthew 15:19).

Nothing we have ever done has been out of character. All of our moral and spiritual decisions come from our hearts. When life is easy, we can couch our words and catch our mistakes. But when the pressure of the wilderness bears upon us, our true nature comes spilling out just as it did with the Israelites. It's in these times that we discover who we truly are on the inside.

If we possess a spirit of fear, then fear will come out. If a critical spirit lives within us, then we will be critical. If our hearts are self-centered, then our response to the wilderness will be all about ourselves. If we are angry or bitter, that's what will come to the surface.

Think about a wilderness experience you have had recently or may be experiencing now. What did it tell you about yourself? Did it reveal that you are controlled by fear—the fear of confrontation, the fear of failure, or the fear of what others might think? Maybe it confronted you with the reality that what you care about most is your reputation and security. Perhaps it exposed that you care more about being happy than you do about being holy.

As I have spoken on this topic, I have asked people what they have learned about themselves through their wilderness experiences. Here are some common responses:

- I learned that I was full of pride.
- I discovered that I was self-centered and all about me.
- I found out that I thought I could handle everything by myself—and that I couldn't make it through the wilderness that way.

Maybe your wilderness is telling you something very important about your relationship with God. You may talk a big game, but your faith may not be nearly as strong as you thought.

The wilderness is likely to show you some weaknesses and faults you were not fully aware of, but it also can reveal strengths you didn't know you have. You may discover a depth of faith, a strength of character, or a courageous spirit that surprises you.

The wilderness is not your enemy;
it's your friend. It's telling you
exactly what you need
to know about yourself—
where you're strong,
where you're weak,
and where you need to grow
so that you can become
more like Jesus.

A mother of three young children once responded to my request for lessons from the wilderness. I had conducted her husband's funeral after he was killed by a reckless driver who had been drinking. First she wrote about how devastated she felt, saying she could never overcome "the sheer agony of having flesh of my flesh and bone of my bone ripped away." She continued, "Over the next year and a half I learned just how weak and helpless I am. But I have also learned just how strong the Spirit of God is in me."

Your wilderness may reveal that you are much weaker than you ever imagined, but it also may convince you that you are much stronger than you ever dreamed. Either way, it's only under stress that you come face to face with your true self. Under pressure you do not have time to carefully craft your answers and prepare your responses. Under pressure—when the circumstances of life are putting the squeeze on you—what's inside you comes oozing out, unfiltered and unrefined. It's then that you learn who you are and where you are in your relationship with God.

For those of us who want to serve God and be faithful to Christ, what we learn about ourselves in the wilderness is truly important information. When things are going well, we don't tend to think about our lives. We're not as likely to review where we are spiritually or to ask ourselves deep and challenging questions. We can fall into rote patterns that maintain life as we know it. And even if there is some significant flaw or weakness in our character, without stress we can remain oblivious to our true condition. As a result we tend to become comfortable and complacent spiritually and coast in our relationship with God.

If you are content not to grow in your faith, if you don't care whether you know the most important truths about yourself, if you're willing to be the same person you are today thirty years from now, then the last thing in the world you want is a wilderness experience. But if you have decided to live for a spiritual purpose, if you have decided you want to serve God and follow Christ, if you have decided that you want a deeper faith, then the wilderness is not your enemy; it's your friend. It's telling you exactly what you need to know about yourself—where you're strong, where you're weak, and where you need to grow so that you can become more like Jesus.

Sometimes our disappointment and our suffering can be a gift. Sometimes hard times can be good times, because it may take a wilderness to wake us up, make us take a long look in the mirror, and ask ourselves some hard questions.

When we come out of the wilderness, we should have a much better understanding of who we are and where we are in our relationship with God. The flaws and the weaknesses we have discovered should get us off of "autopilot" and cause us to seek God more purposefully than ever. The strengths we have found within ourselves should cause us to face life with a humble confidence like that of the mother of three who learned just how strong the Spirit of God was within her. When you have been through the worst that life can inflict upon you and you have learned that through Christ you can "do all things," you can face future challenges and hardships with a sense of peace and the assurance that God's grace will be sufficient for you.

When you come through the wilderness, you will know what is in your heart, and that is information you have paid a high price to acquire. Make the most of it as you step into the rest that God has promised.

2. The Wilderness Will Change You

Whether your wilderness is a serious illness (yours or that of a loved one), the loss of a job, a divorce, a child or family member with an addiction, a betrayal in business, the death of a spouse or a child, or some other difficult experience, how you make your way through it will change you. You will always come out of the wilderness different than when you went in. You will be stronger or weaker, full of faith or full of doubts, closer to God or further away, more conformed to the image of Christ or more self-centered. Your heart will have been softened or your spirit will have become cynical and bitter.

It's easy to let the wilderness change us for the worse. That requires no faith, no effort, no intentionality, and no strength. When we suffer, we have a tendency to turn inward instead of outward. It's so easy to say, "I shouldn't have to suffer like this. No one understands. No one knows how I feel. No one really cares."

If the pain is great enough and the loss is devastating enough, some of us shut down and give up. We quit looking up to God and stop reaching out to others. We hide from life in the darkness of despair. We live alone in a desert of self-pity. We crawl into a bottle or something else that promises to take away our pain, but it only takes us away from those who love us. Emotionally and sometimes physically, we run away from everyone who cares and from every reminder of what life once was or what we had hoped it might be. And we die inside.

Long after the struggle is over and our circumstances have changed for the better, we can leave the wilderness but not truly step into that place of rest that God has promised. We may return to the normalcy of life but our spirit has become angry and bitter—or maybe it's simply numb and unfeeling. We stop believing that God cares for us, that each day is a gift, and that life can be good again.

You see, it's possible for us to come out of the wilderness but for the wilderness to remain in us. We return to the normalcy of life, but we remain devastated emotionally and spiritually. Fatalism now lives where once there was faith. Cynicism has replaced compassion. Even among friends we feel alone. Instead of being open with others we feel a need to protect ourselves and hide who we are inside.

It's possible for the devastation of the wilderness to remain within our souls much longer than it needs to, but that's never God's will for our lives. He wants us to allow the wilderness to change us for the better. And it can.

In his work *How the Irish Saved Civilization*, Thomas Cahill shares an account of an Irishman who was changed for the better.[1] He sets the stage by explaining that around the year A.D. 401, the Roman Empire was crumbling, and barbarian tribes from neighboring lands were growing in strength and threatening the security of Rome itself.

Troops were called from faraway provinces to fight battles closer to home.

No longer safeguarded by the legions as it had been before, the province of Britannia seemed a prize without protection, and it began to be plundered and ravaged by barbarian raiders. Not only were crops and livestock stolen, but human beings were also taken and enslaved.

"In the slavery business, no tribe was fiercer or more feared than the Irish."[2] Often they came in small raiding parties in the dark of night, silently stealing sleeping children from their parents. They also came in larger war parties, and on at least one occasion they seized thousands of young prisoners who were sold in the slave markets of Ireland.

One of those taken by the Celts was a sixteen-year-old boy named Patricius. He was the son of nobility with a bright future awaiting him. His grandfather had been a Catholic priest, and his father was a tax collector. Taken from the order and security he had known all his life, he was transported to a dark, illiterate land where he did not speak the language or understand the customs. The people there were uncivilized and superstitious. They worshiped the many gods of the druids.[3]

The Celts were a wild and brutal people. Human sacrifice was not unheard of. Warriors would wear the heads of their victims dangling from their belts. Tales were even told of their women's ferocious victories in battle. Patricius could hardly have landed in a more foreign and frightening place.

Patricius became the property of a warlord named Miliucc, whom he served as a shepherd-slave. At times he worked with other slaves. At other times he was by himself in the wilderness, watching the sheep—his only companions hunger, nakedness, and loneliness. He tells us in his writings that never before had he paid attention to religion. He didn't really believe in God, and he thought priests to be foolish. But now in the midst of impossible circumstances, he turned to the God of his parents and began to pray. He prayed constantly day and night, even in the midst of snow, frost, and rain because, as he wrote, "the Spirit within me was ardent."[4]

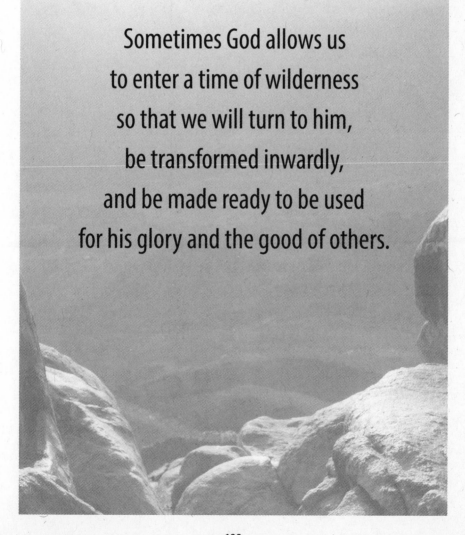

Sometimes God allows us
to enter a time of wilderness
so that we will turn to him,
be transformed inwardly,
and be made ready to be used
for his glory and the good of others.

Patricius endured six years of suffering and slavery. During this wilderness period he was changed. Now in his early twenties, he had been transformed from a careless boy into a man who walked with God.

After his six years of suffering, a voice told him in a dream, "Your hungers are rewarded: you are going home....Look, your ship is ready."[5] Cahill notes that Patricius set out, walking some two hundred miles without being stopped or followed. Finally he reached a southeastern inlet where he saw his ship. When he approached the captain and asked to join the crew, he was rejected and sent away at first; but then the sailors called him back and allowed him to sign on as a hired hand.

Eventually Patricius returned to his family, who embraced him and begged him never to leave them again. But Patricius had been changed by his time in the wilderness. His mind and body had been steeled by years of suffering. His spirit had been softened and made alive by years alone with God.

Time passed, and one night while safe in bed in the home of his childhood, he saw in a dream a large multitude of Irish in a forest he remembered, calling out to him: "We beg you to come and walk among us once more."[6]

The visions continued until Christ himself spoke to Patricius, and he answered the call. He spent years studying the Christian faith, learning theology, and doing the work of a priest. But eventually he returned to the land of his captivity.

Over the next thirty years, Patricius preached the gospel and taught the ways of God to the Irish who had mistreated him. He showed a particular concern for those who were enslaved as he once had been. Through his work, Ireland was transformed. Thousands came to know Christ. Slavery was ended. The constant warring between the many tribes diminished. The dark and devilish druid gods that once terrorized a superstitious people were largely dethroned and defanged and replaced by a God of grace.

You know Patricius, of course, but by another name. You know him by the name he was given when he was made a bishop: Patrick, the patron saint of Ireland.

Patricius spent six years in a frightening wilderness of loneliness and suffering. But it was the wilderness that prepared him for the work that would bring life to people lost in darkness. So much of what he experienced when he was a slave in Ireland made him able to minister to the Irish like no one else could. He learned their language, their customs, and their superstitions. He learned about their gods. He came to understand their hopes and their fears. Because of his time in the wilderness, when the opportunity came he was able to present Christ to the Irish in a way that would speak to the depths of their hearts.

Patricius would have learned none of these things had he not gone through the most difficult time of his life. What seemed like wasted years in a dark wilderness of confusion and pain were the very years when God was preparing him to be used in a unique and powerful way.

There was something even more important that the wilderness did for Patricius. It is what the experience of being enslaved and alone did to change his heart. Torn from his family and having everything he depended upon taken from him, Patricius had nowhere to go but to God. As we have seen, that's what difficult times can do for us—and sometimes it is what they're meant to do. Sometimes God allows us to enter a time of wilderness so that we will turn to him, be transformed inwardly, and be made ready to be used for his glory and the good of others.

Looking back on his time of enslavement, Patrick wrote: "God used the time to shape and mold me into something better. He made me into what I am now—someone very different from what I once was, someone who can care about others and work to help them. Before I was a slave, I didn't even care about myself."[7]

We all will go through difficult, devastating experiences. We will lose something or someone important to us. We will make mistakes we think we can't recover from. We will hurt others and find ourselves isolated from people we love and need. We will be misunderstood and misjudged and betrayed. We will have experiences that break our hearts and crush our spirits.

It is in these wilderness experiences that God can make us into someone very different, someone more like Christ, as he did with Patricius. The most difficult days of our lives can be the times when we learn to trust God in a new way and to care more deeply for others who are suffering and needy.

Yes, we all will go through the wilderness. And we will come out of the wilderness different than when we entered. There's no question about that. The only question is whether our pain and confusion will turn us away from God so that we leave the wilderness angry, bitter, and cynical; or whether we will turn to God and say, "I am lost; come find me. I am weak; give me strength. I am broken; put my life back together so I become the person you want me to be." If we choose the latter, we can leave the wilderness closer to God, stronger in our faith, and ready to be used to bring life and hope to others.

3. The Wilderness Will Give You a Gift to Share

It's human nature to believe that what we have to offer to others is primarily our knowledge and our expertise. We think we will make a difference in the lives of others based on our strengths and our successes. But I have come to believe that what most profoundly impacts the lives of others is what we have learned from our struggles and failures.

In recent years I have observed that after I preach on Sunday morning or speak at our church's men's group, often someone (usually older) will say to me, "I wish I had heard you say that thirty years ago." My standard reply is, "I hadn't made enough mistakes thirty years ago to teach what you heard today."

It's true. Thirty years ago I hadn't failed enough to teach much of what I know today. You may have heard the story about a young man who asked the CEO of his company how he became CEO. The older man said, "By making good decisions." The young man asked, "How did you learn to make good decisions?" The CEO said, "Through experience." The young man asked again, "And how did you get experience?" The CEO responded, "By making bad decisions."

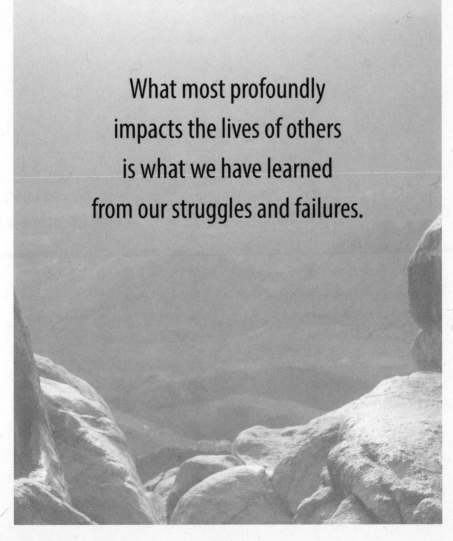

What most profoundly
impacts the lives of others
is what we have learned
from our struggles and failures.

Over my thirty years in ministry, I can't count how many mistakes I've made. But what matters most is what I've learned from them. I've not only made mistakes, I have suffered. Though my suffering does not compare to that of some, like many I have struggled with depression. My wife, Peggy, and I know the pain and the helplessness of having a loved one addicted to drugs. We also have experienced the terrible stress that puts on a marriage. And as a pastor, I live with great sorrow for people I love who have cancer, who have lost children, and who have walked away from God.

What I have to offer to others who are hurting is not a sermon on "Seven Secrets for Successful Living" or stories of how well I did when life was hard. What I have to offer, in addition to the truths of God's Word, is what I've learned from my own hard experiences. What makes our lives powerful—not just impressive but powerful—is the authenticity that comes from having suffered and struggled. What makes our words impactful—not just interesting or thought-provoking but impactful—is the authority that results from having come to the end of ourselves and being able to say that God was faithful.

When you have been devastated by life but have come out of that wilderness strong of spirit and soft of heart, that's when you will be able to minister life and hope to others who are hurting—and with great power and grace. Tell people about your strengths, and they may think they're not as strong as you. But tell them about your weaknesses, and they will listen because they will see themselves in you. Tell people about your victories, and they may be impressed. But tell them about the God who was with you in your failures, and they will be encouraged.

For hurting people, what is always more comforting and healing than the right answer is someone who understands and cares. The wilderness prepares us to be that person for others. When we remember how we struggled, when we remember how long our nights were and how nothing eased our agony, when we remember how alone we felt, when we remember that doing all the right things and praying all the right prayers still left us empty and in pain— that's when we can give other hurting souls the most important gift of being with them, not only physically but also emotionally and spiritually. And knowing they're not alone can be enough to get them through the most difficult time of their life.

Recently someone said to me, "It must be very hard when you have to comfort someone who has lost a child or a spouse." It is terribly difficult. It's not a task I ever look forward to.

When I was a young pastor, as I prepared to visit a family who had experienced a tragic death, I would pray for God to give me the right words to say. My heart was right, but I was so naive. I must have thought that if I could just say the right thing or come up with the right answer, then I could remove the pain inside a grieving heart and take away the loss of a loved one.

When I was pastoring in Atlanta, Texas, I went to visit one of our older members in the hospital. Before I got there, another couple had already arrived and were visiting with him. The Curries. You'd love them. Everybody did. They were retired, full of life and faith, always smiling and laughing, obviously still in love, and constantly helping others.

In the course of our conversation, someone mentioned the Curries' son. I knew they had a son and a daughter, but they spoke of this son as if he had passed away. So I asked if he had, and they responded that their son had been "the All-American kid"—popular, a great student, and a star athlete. But he struggled with depression. When he was still a teenager, he took his own life.

I was absolutely stunned. I tried to put it together. They had suffered a terrible loss, but they were living such full, beautiful lives.

Then I said something stupid. I asked, "So, how long does it take to get over something like that?" Almeta looked at me kindly, thank God, and she said, "Well, of course, you never do."

There are some pains, some questions, some losses that we never really get over. We have to live with them. But we can live lives that are full and that bless others if, even while we carry our loss, we know that we are not alone and that God is with us.

Through that experience and others, I've learned that my words can't heal people. My "brilliant answers" will never take away another person's pain. But I also have learned that I do not have to walk into a dark home where hearts are hurting and be the answer. I just have to go into the darkness and be there with them. I just have to hurt with them and cry with them and wonder why with them. I just have to make it okay for them to ask whatever they need to ask, become as angry as they need to be, and weep as much as they need to weep. I just have to listen to them, love them, and in some small way be the presence of God with them. Then healing can begin. That's how people get better. That's how they become whole. Someone loves them, and in that love they feel the love of God. Someone is "with them" in their pain and their questions, and in that presence they feel the presence of Immanuel, God with us. Even if they don't have all the answers, they have the assurance of God's presence; and that is enough. In fact, it's more than all the answers in the world.

The wilderness will give you a gift to share if you allow it to do so. It can make your heart tender to the suffering of others. It can fill your spirit with a depth of compassion you never would have known without your own time of devastation. It can teach you that you don't have to be the answer; you just have to be present with another person.

As you leave the wilderness, look for others who are there now. There is no greater gift you can give, no greater comfort you can provide than truly being with someone who is hurting. And there is no better place to learn the lessons of compassion than in the wilderness of your own suffering.

The wilderness is always devastating. It brings us to the end of ourselves so that we can have a new beginning with God. Its stress can reveal to us who we are and where we need to grow. Its challenges can change us into people who are stronger in faith and closer to God. Its pain can give us a gift to share with others who are lost and alone.

Whatever it may be, the wilderness in your life *will* end. You will come out. As the author of Hebrews tells us, the promise of entering God's rest still stands. There is a place of peace and a time of joy waiting for you. God has promised it to you. My prayer is that when you leave the wilderness, you'll be able to say, "I wouldn't go through that again for a million dollars, but I wouldn't take all the money in the world for what I learned about walking with God."

You will not be the same person when you leave the wilderness, and that can be an incredible gift. There is a way to go through the wilderness that will transform your life in the most wonderful way, leaving you closer to God, more like his Son Jesus, stronger in your faith, and more equipped to be a blessing to others who are hurting. It will not be easy. But it will be worth it.

Notes

Chapter 1: No Way Around the Wilderness

1. *Yeshimon* or *Jehimon*, http://www.abarim-publications.com
   /Meaning/Jeshimon.html#.VN9eOtgtF9Awww.abarim
   -publication.com.
2. M. Scott Peck, *The Road Less Traveled: A New Psychology of Love,
   Traditional Values and Spiritual Growth* (New York: Simon and
   Schuster, 1978), 15.
3. Associated Press Wire Staff, "Adv. Army Medic Reassures
   Teddy, Jr.," Associated Press Wire Service, December 4, 1973,
   as seen in *The Kansas City Times*, http://www.newspapers.com
   /newspage/50264759/.
4. Theodore Roosevelt. "American Ideals." Address at Proceedings
   of the Fifty-fifth Annual Session of the Iowa State Teachers
   Association, Des Moines, Iowa, November 4, 1910.
5. "Mega Millions Lottery Could Make You More Likely To Go
   Bankrupt," Alexander Eichler, *The Huffington Post*, March 30,
   2012, http://www.huffingtonpost.com/2012/03/30/mega
   -millions-lottery-bankrupt_n_1392414.html.

Chapter 2: Entering the Wilderness

1. Tim Sledge, *Making Peace with Your Past: Help for Adult Children of
   Dysfunctional Families* (Nashville: LifeWay Press, 1991).
2. "How Firm a Foundation," *The United Methodist Hymnal*
   (Nashville: The United Methodist Publishing House, 1989), 529,
   stanza 3.

Chapter 3: Walking with Others in the Wilderness

1. Scholars have debated whether Hobab was Moses' brother-in-law (Numbers 10:29) or father-in-law (Judges 4:11).
2. U2. "Sometimes You Can't Make It on Your Own." *How to Dismantle an Atomic Bomb*. Island/Interscope Records, 2004. CD.
3. "Free at Last," http://www.negrospirituals.com/songs/free_at _last_from.htm

Chapter 4: Walking with God in the Wilderness

1. Maya Angelou, *I Know Why the Caged Bird Sings* (New York: Random House, 1979), 23.

Chapter 5: Avoiding Wrong Turns in the Wilderness

1. *Manna*, http://biblehub.com/greek/3131.htm.

Chapter 6: Coming Out of the Wilderness

1. Thomas Cahill, *How the Irish Saved Civilization: The Untold Story of Ireland's Heroic Role from the Fall of Rome to the Rise of Medieval Europe* (New York: Anchor Books, 1995).
2. Ibid., 37.
3. Ibid.; read Patricius's story beginning on page 37.
4. Ibid., 102.
5. Ibid., 102–103.
6. Ibid., 105.
7. Philip Freeman, *St. Patrick of Ireland: A Biography* (New York: Simon & Schuster, 2004), 29.